"Wow what an inspiration! Nothing happens 'till a sale is made and Alex sure sold me.

Business--in fact capitalism--is built on this principal "find a need and fill it or take a current service or product, look at it, and find a way to make it BETTER".

Alex is a great example of what makes America great;, he's young, has fire in the belly to make it better and that will lead to better money every time."

~**David Hofmann,** *Stock Trader/Investor/Humanitarian*

"Welcome to the road least travelled. While many other young men his age are satisfied with video games, sports and other recreational activities of their age - Alex has converted a challenging time in our country's history into a productive one for himself with the writing of THE BIG IDEA. In this book he has applied the basics of entrepreneurship that make our country the amazing place that it is.

Alex, you stand head and shoulders above the men of your age and I'm excited for your future. Thank you for being you- resourceful and a servant leader. In being that, you are prepared for life! Bravo!"

~**Lou Sandoval, Chicago, IL -** *Entrepreneur | Builder of Businesses, Brands and High Performing Teams*

"Alex...

What an aspiring Entrepreneur you are! From what I've read about your terrific rise in helping kids in the medical arena....I can already say you have the required qualifications to be a very successful entrepreneur!

Alex, it took me until my mid 30's to accomplish what you are already doing as a young teen entrepreneur!

After trying to get a franchise for 7 years, and hearing "No", by several franchisers, by being PERSISTENT, I was finally awarded 1 franchise restaurant. Afterwards, I owned and operated 27 franchised restaurants, 1,300 employees, and $25 million in annual revenues. Little Caesars, Applebee's, On The Border and Burger King. At your age, and entrepreneurial spirit and intelligence, you have the talent to overtake Jeff Bezos from Amazon in your lifetime!

From one entrepreneur to another...stay the course and even if it takes longer than expected...it's YOUR DREAM...DON'T LET ANYONE TAKE IT AWAY! BE PERSISTENT!

Godspeed..."

~Tony Álvarez, *San Antonio, Texas CEO/Social Entrepreneur*

THE BiG iDEA

THE ROADMAP TO ENTREPRENEURSHIP

ALEX JIMÉNEZ

THE BiG iDEA

For more information, visit:
www.alexjimenez.biz

Fig Factor Media, LLC | www.figfactormedia.com
Cover Design & Layout by Juan Manuel Serna
Printed in the United States of America

FIG FACTOR MEDIA

ISBN: 978-1-952779-17-6
Library of Congress Control Number: 2020917982

This book is dedicated to my biggest mentor (dad).

TABLE OF CONTENTS

ACKNOWLEDGMENTS

I want to thank all my supporters along the way from start to finish: Tia Sammy, Grandparents, and my amazing mom.

INTRODUCTION: WAKE UP

WAKE UP! Yes you. Every day of your life you wake up, go to school, go home, eat, go with your family, and then... BAM! The same cycle happens again and again and again! This is the life of MILLIONS of people around the world. Not only their life but their mentality and habits.

Schools, our parents, teachers, friends, news, TV, and so much more makes us believe that's the way of life. They tell you when to have your vacation, when to go to work, when to be with your family, and when this or that.

It's sad to see hundreds of thousands of children around the world being brainwashed by the school system to have the belief that you NEED to have a 9 to 5 job to live happily and to provide for yourself. "The Bigger the Degree, the Bigger the Key" (Key referring to a house key) is what my middle school teacher would always tell me and my peers. Not only my schoolteachers, but almost everyone around me told me the same thing over and over again. Even though you might be going through the same thing in your life right now, there's always a way to keep yourself from becoming another one of the world's workers.

In this book, you'll find out how I, and others like me, refused to be taken over by the "Matrix" and be pulled into the worker mindset at a very young age. You'll find out what entrepreneurship is, the basics of it, how you can become one yourself, and even read stories of how entrepreneurs escaped the rat race.

This book is dedicated to people of all ages, but if you're a young teen to a young adult that's either in college or high school, then this book is for you especially. Think of this book as a way to get your feet wet, and to KNOW that being an employee is not the only option for you. If you're in college right now and start to think that school isn't going to help you in the future and start to think that you might want to start a business, then this book is great for you. If you're about to graduate high school and are debating whether or not you want pursue college, this book is what you need. If you're a teenager and want to know how a business works, how to be an entrepreneur, and the do's and don'ts of it; this is what you need.

You might be thinking to yourself, "Why should I read this book? This kid doesn't know what he's talking about." That's fine. I'm not here to convince you to that I'm the "real deal". Before you judge anyone or anything, it's best to know what they have been through or what they've done. I'm not a millionaire kid or even the smartest kid in the room, but what I do know is how to run a company efficiently from a kid's standpoint as well as a professional adult view. My company, Smiles Against Cancer (I'll refer to it as SAC) is a non-profit organization that strives to put a smile on every kid's face that has cancer (www.smilesagainstcancer.org). Since 2017, my dad and I have been growing SAC as much as possible. Were currently reach two states and started from one hospital. We went from donating only about 25 toys to last year donating nearly 1,000! Although I'm only 13 years old, I'm always trying to find new ways to improve my business skills to the point where I believe I can help other teens to improve, or at least understand how to run a business. I also know I can help other teenagers become entrepreneurs.

On the other hand, one of my podcasts, The Big Idea, has been up for a couple of months and in the first month we grew from 0 to over 5,000 listeners! How? I've committed myself to use everything I've written in this book in all of my businesses/organizations.

In every book, whatever subject it may be, you can almost always find golden nuggets on that subject. On whatever it may be. In this book I want you to know that whenever there's a golden nugget I'll let you know by giving it a **BOLD** font. Whenever you see a bolded sentence, write it down and take notes on it because it may be the exact thing you need in your life right now.

This book is written for everyone that is getting a start in business, and for people who want to take action. Action is something you'll be reading about frequently in this book. I can't stress enough how important taking action is, not only in creating your business, but in life. If you want to create something new that never been done before, you can't just pray and hope that your idea is going to create itself without any effort. You have to take action in whatever you need to have happen. You need to pay for rent? Take action. You don't have money for that new computer you want? Take action. You want to live in a beautiful home near the ocean, surrounded by palm trees, doing whatever makes you happy? STOP DREAMING ABOUT IT AND TAKE ACTION.

I want you to keep one thing in mind while reading this, take something new that you learned and apply it to your life. Entrepreneurship isn't for everyone, so don't feel like this book is misleading if you have different beliefs, and don't feel obligated to read this. This is your choice. In the words of Jim Rohn, **"Formal education will make you a living; self-education will make you a fortune."**

CHAPTER ONE

THE NEED TO CHANGE

"If you do what you've always done, you'll get what you've always gotten." ~Tony Robbins

_____

CHANGE THE PEOPLE YOU'RE WITH THE MOST

YOU HAVE TO CHANGE! While I will talk about various subjects of entrepreneurship and the many ways how to become one, it is a necessity to have the will and courage to change, not only mentally, but socially.

"Birds of a feather flock together" is what Les Brown said in one of his keynotes. (He was first introduced by William Turner). This quote was the defining moment for many multi-millionaires and billionaires.

This quote should be applied to everyone and anyone. In the quote the birds represent you. The second part (the feather) represents the people you go out with the most-your best friends, your family, your partner. The third part is the key meaning of the quote, "Birds of a feather **flock together.**" Birds flocking together means the habits of the people you hang out with will start to rub off on you.

For example, if you start to hang out with people who hit the gym daily, you have a higher chance of going to the gym more often. In a study done by the University of Michigan, they surveyed the number of students that vape each year. What they discovered was shocking; the number of teenagers who vape more than DOUBLED in only two years. In fact, the number of 10th graders that admitted to vaping increased from eight to 20 percent.

One of the interviewers asked a freshman in high school,

"Who or what made you start vaping?" He answered, "I don't know what started it. I mean it kinda just happened, I guess it was because my friends did." As they asked more kids the same question, "What made you start to vape?" an astonishing 39 percent or almost three million students vape due to their friends, family, and who they are with the most. That is only one of many examples of how people are influenced by their friends, peers, and family.

Obviously, we've come a long way on how we interact with people. **There are THOUSANDS of ways we can interact and meet new people! Think about it, you can meet people in ways others didn't before. Even in the little things--social media, dating apps, walks with your dog, while talking to people during everyday activities, saying hi to the mail man, texts, face time, school, your job,** FaceBook groups, social clubs, and even Cosplay events. There are so many ways you can meet people and have them influence your life without you knowing.

For example, let's say you're a HUGE MCU (Marvel Cinematic Universe) fan, and one day you scroll down in Instagram and see an ad about a Disney expo that's going to release everything about all their new and upcoming movies, TV shows, and games. You end up meeting another huge MCU fan and find out you have a bunch of similarities and you exchange numbers. A week later you meet them again just to talk and have a drink. You go through the whole day talking about what you both like, your interests. They convince you to go to a club meeting at their local church, and while you're hesitant, you go. After the club is over, you end up loving it and want to go again. You continue going and pretty soon you realize you've been going there almost every week. Of course this is just an example but the lesson here is that **you can easily meet someone and they end up getting you into a habit of going to a place or trying something different, either for the better or worse.**

Who do you think some of the wealthiest people in the world are surrounded with? None of them hang out with people who are below them, and in many cases with people who are at their same level. They are all connected one way or another.

Larry Ellison is best known for wanting to take out his competition, and being the founder and CEO of Oracle. He once talked about how he and Steve Jobs became good friends when Jobs was kicked out of Apple and he was in the early stages of Next, a company he started after getting kicked out of Apple. They talked about how Jobs might regain the title of CEO at Apple, and how things were at Pixar. At one point, Ellison offered the idea of buying Apple out and making Jobs the CEO. Jobs declined, saying he wanted to save Apple by making them acquire Next, and then joining the board. The point is that wealthy people stick together and give each other ideas. At times it's not even about making more money. Maybe they just want to help each other solve problems.

There are many billionaires that you might not have known are friends with other billionaires. For instance, Elon Musk (CEO of SpaceX and Tesla) is friends with Larry Page and Sergey Brin (co-founders of Google), Mark Zuckerberg (co-founder of Facebook), and Drew Houston (CEO of Dropbox).Some otherwell-known friendships include Bill Gates (co-founder of Microsoft) and Warren Buffet (CEO of Berkshire Hathaway), Jack Dorsey (CEO of Twitter) and Kevin Systrom (co-founder of Instagram), and Elon Musk with Larry Ellison.

Many others are friends with each other and benefit one another. Even in the medieval times, when there were queens and kings living in the 15th century. I'm sure you've seen those cliché movies and TV shows that have presented the idea that all the poor people had to be with the poor people while the rich and wealthy people had to stick together and marry each other, and it's true. It would be nearly forbidden to marry or have any type of relationship with people outside of your social group. Today we still have those social groups who think that you can only be with people that have the same things as you.

The majority of people who, for instance, like the Bulls basketball team are most likely going to stay with that team for their life and hang out with people who also love the Bulls team. The same thing applies to you. Think about a hobby you like besides business. Now that you have your hobby, think about your friends that like the same hobby. In this case, you reading this book means you're either someone who's an entrepreneur, is starting a business, a teenager, or someone who doesn't know much about business. **If you want to be successful in the thing you want to achieve or in a business you want to create, you need to surround yourself with those who share your idea.** As I said earlier there are hundreds of ways you can find people with your common interests very easily and quickly.

I want you to try an experiment that will show you that you can easily be changed by people you are with, and if it'll benefit you. All you need is a phone, something you want to achieve (a goal), and the ability to accept that you're not the best while having the will to learn. Pick something you'd like to do in your life--short-term or long-term. It could be anything you want--from being a professional cook to being a pilot to making your business expand to making more customers.

Once you have that idea/goal you want to achieve in your mind, I want you to go to Facebook, Instagram, Tictok, or any social media platform you have that has an option to Direct Message (DM). Next, you're going to search for "best *(your goal)* in *(your town)*" and DM every single person that pops up (that's real or has a good reputation) this:

Hey _____, I'm a big fan of your work and I'm aspiring to become a _____. I'm _____ and I want an opportunity to learn from you as much as I can. I'm willing to

*help you with anything _____ related you need me to do.
I'll work for free; the only thing I would like in return is to be
able to consume all the education of _____ you can give
me. I want to learn as much _____ I can while from you
now and in the future. If you have any questions about me or
in general feel free to DM me back on _____.*

After, send them the message and wait for a response. Next, copy and paste this to all of the people you find and wait until someone replies. Obviously, you would like to change your writing and change it up a bit. This concept to DM people is extremely useful. Many other entrepreneurs say that this is a great way to reach people you want to learn from, especially Gary Vaynerchuk. I'm betting if you search up "Gary Vee DM people" on Google you'll find countless videos of him saying to DM people and learn from them.

I know I'm about to get a lot of people saying that they can't just leave and learn from someone at random, or they have other priorities. That's fine. When I wrote that script, I tried to make it as changeable as possible. For those of you who have a family or are in school, you don't need to learn from them directly. You can change the script to ask if you can learn from them through Skype, phone, FaceTime, or email. Of course, you can't just expect them to reply to you, especially if they're someone well known. So, an alternative, and a better chance to make them notice you, is to send them something that will help them while showing the reason you have the ability to help and learn from them.

For example, if you wanted to become an artist and the person you DM is Travis Scott, than make a sample or even a full song with his songs beats and voice. Maybe you would want to send them a remix of their song, make a new beat, or a lyric that they might be able to use for a song. Something to get their attention that is quality filled. I don't mean to make the sound quality perfect; what I mean is to make what you did for them quality in itself. Make it as great as you can, and make it different from others.

The same thing goes with any other artist, musician, cook, actor, etc. If you want to become a cook then DM a cook that knows what he's doing, has a good reputation, and who's legit. Do the same thing and try to figure out what can help them in what they're doing and give it to them for free. Do this and you'll most likely find someone who will help you. This technique obviously requires more work than a random thing you read in a book, but if you are willing to learn, and want to learn something to make your dream possible, then it's worth it. If you are on the fence about trying it because of other things you have to worry about, then it's fine, I understand. However, if you truly do have the opportunity to make your dream happen, and to learn from others, then do it, take the chance, and take the risk.

Going back to the subject of surrounding yourself with others who impact your life, habits, and mentality for better or worse, an example of this is Jay-Z. In the height of his career he was surrounded with "rich and famous" people almost all the time. Not that it was bad at that time, because he could've gotten many song ideas, or maybe he was just having fun, but despite him being with his friends, they didn't have something that Jay-Z latter discovered in his career—the wealthy mentality. A good majority of athletes, singers, actors, and TV personalities have gone from broke to rich to broke again because they never understood, or never learned, the rich man's mentality. **They go broke not because they spend too much or lend money to people; they go broke because they never learned how to make their money compound. They never learned how to leave the poor mentality, the bad influences (like friends) that never helped them, and instead dragged him or her down to the level they never were supposed to be in the first place.**

Back to Jay-Z. He's written songs that have been a massive success both critically and financially, which made him a lot of money. He could've gone all over the world, bought a house, given away, or even spent everything in one shot with his money. He did do a couple of things on that list, however instead of spending everything in one shot without any financial knowledge he studied or at least learned the rich man mentality. He could've been broke right now living a bad life and losing it all, but instead he became the first billionaire rapper/singer. He went from 200 million to a billion dollars! **Why? It all came down to one thing, surrounding himself with wealthy people which allowed him to have a rich man mentality.**

One of Jay-Z's quotes also shows perfectly why being with the people that have a poor-person mentality does change you. He said, **"A wise man once told me, don't argue with fools. Cause people from a distance can't tell who is who."** The point is, why waste your time with others that don't help you reach your dreams and goals?

Another example of people surrounding themselves with wealthy people who did change them is Kobe Bryant (RIP). Before he passed, he became very familiar with business and how to invest his wealth. After he retired from the MBA, he started to learn how to become even wealthier than he was at that time. He mentioned regularly that he would call business people and entrepreneurs to ask them how they made it or the secrets to success.

Chris Sacca, another sucessesful entreprenuer, was in an interview with Bill Simmons and mentioned that in the middle of the night he would get texts or calls from Kobe about an article he might've read or a Ted Talk on a subject Kobe didn't know about. He was dedicated and willing to surround himself with people that could help him with his goals and business in the future as well as the present. He surrounded himself with people that helped him with his goals and dreams, not people that brought him down or people that were partying all the time and not caring about their wealth.

Many others, such as Michael Jordan, have learned the rich mentality. He went from having a gambling addiction and spending most of his money, to becoming one of the very few athlete billionaires in the world, and creating one of the most recognizable brands in the WORLD (Air Jordan's)! Another artist that ended up understanding that he didn't need jewelry or name brands to impress his friends is 21 Savage. He doesn't hang out with others who might want to be with him for what he has, or people that don't help him become wealthier. Instead, he trades the majority of his jewelry for real estate, crypto currency, and into businesses, according to his manger. He is also interested in inspiring young minds and artists on their journey.

If you have friends that are losers, party every week, or pull you down in your journey instead of pulling you up, get rid of them. **Have the courage to leave them behind and start to make a change in your life. Surround yourself with people that have done what you want to accomplish and follow them. In other words, find a group of people (or a mentor) and learn from them and shadow them.** If you have friends or family that is against entrepreneurship you don't have to push them away or disagree with them, just make the decision to apply what you've learned in this book.

No, it's not going to be as easy as it seems, and it never will be, but think about the people you hang out with like this: pretend you're a wolf that was just born; you grow up with your pack while being trained on all the basics of survival, how to eat, live, and hunt; and you grow to be the most respected leader in your pack while being the biggest and strongest. How did you become the best wolf? By surrounding yourself with other wolves that were strong, fearless, and great leaders since you were a baby cub.

Here's another scenario. The same thing happens - you're born a healthy cub with your pack, but instead of growing up with your pack and surrounding yourself with other strong wolves, one day you get lost and end up finding yourself with little sheep. Years go by and you're taught how to eat, live, and hide. You grow up to be part of the crowd while running away from other wolf packs. One day, you wake up to find you and your sheep friends being attacked. You run in circles not being able to escape the other wolves, and you see all the sheep killed one by one until you're the only one left. You're a little sheep and going against the leader of the pack, and, well, you know the rest.

This is a metaphor on how surrounding yourself with others does impact you and your life. **If you hang out with little sheep, you'll end up being in the little sheep pack, but if you want to be a strong wolf then surround yourself with other strong wolves.**

Someone who perfectly explains why you need to change the people you're hanging with is motivational speaker, Jim Rohn. He said, "Show me your friends and I'll show you your future." That quote is the perfect way to explain what this part of the chapter is about. Who you spend the most time with is who you're going to become. I know that I've been on this subject for a while, but the importance of knowing this is huge. Just as Rohn says - friends=future.

MENTALITY

YES! You got one part of the equation. You've started to hang out with more people that are helping you to get where you want to be in your life. Now what? The next part that you have to change about yourself is your mentality. You've probably heard someone say something close to this. "Come on, be happy. You need to change that attitude to a positive one." Or maybe they said, "If you keep that attitude, you'll have it for the rest of your days." Maybe it was your parents, or maybe it was a teacher, but it's true. **If you have a bad attitude toward something, you'll have that attitude for a while. If you say to yourself that you can't do something or that something is impossible, you'll end up having a hard time making that thing work.**

Let's do an experiment. What this experiment will prove, is that talking negatively about yourself does affect you in a big way. Get your phone, turn on your camera, and record yourself making two videos. On one video, record yourself saying only positive stuff. Like, "You'll get there. You're the best. Don't worry about anything, keep it going." After you record the first video, make another video recording yourself only saying negative stuff. Such as, "I'm bad at my job. I suck. This isn't meant for me." Every day for half a month and then play back the audio with only the negative words, once a day, every day.

After a couple of days, you'll see how the negative video affects you. It could affect your mood, yourself esteem, or how you talk to people. When half a month of listening to the negative audio goes by, play the positive video. Something different should be happening. After a couple of days listening to the positive video, your mood should start to change, but for the better. You might start to say nice things to your friends or maybe you might be happier. At the end of the month listing to the positive video, you should be happier or more positive in your day-to-day life. I've done this myself, and it did start to affect me. Even if you don't want to do it for a month, just do it for a day. It truly does change you and proves that your mood and self-esteem does get affected by what you say to yourself.

Once you get your mentality fixed into the right mindset, you have to keep it for the rest of your day, week, month, year, and life. Ok, not for the whole year but at least for the time you need. You have to keep that mentality throughout your day. Think about it yourself, if you're pumped up for the day and ready to take anything on, but slowly lose that mentality, then why are you even making yourself seem that you're ready for anything? Keep that mentality whenever you feel like you're going to give up or you can't take the pain and suffering. No, it's not going to be as easy as just telling yourself that you're going to keep going. In fact, the most important thing to do whenever you feel you're going to give up is to take action on getting yourself into a better state of mind.

Your state of mind is very susceptible to change, even the time you spend on things. Your phone, tablet, laptop, TV, as well as any other devices you have, can change your mind for both better and worse. Take your phone, for example, and look at what you watch on your phone. Do you use it for business only? Do you use it simply to make and receive calls? Maybe you use it for games only, or maybe you use it for social media and for your friends. Whatever it may be you're using that device for, you're most likely to have a harder time seeing and using your device for something else.

If you use your phone strictly for business-related things and nothing else, you'll have a harder time learning and enjoying social media. Vise versa if you use your phone mainly for social media and to talk to friends--you'll have a harder time using your phone for business-related things and business-related calls. If you dive even deeper, you can even find out that the people you follow gets you to act differently and more how they act.

Think about it, everyday you take in and see all the things they do. If they post content that talks about politics and what they think about a certain type of candidate, you may favor them. Then, if your friends follow people that are against that candidate, and are following the competitor, you're most likely to vote for him or her.

In another scenario, if you follow someone who posts

daily content that's positive, inspiring, or motivating, then you're going to have that positive mindset in your head, and in your day. It's simple—who you follow, and who you look up to, is the person you're most likely going to take your habits from. I'd like to say that this is why many kids and their parents have conflicts with each other, from a kid's perspective. Kids and their parents aren't going to have the same goals and opinions on things.

Back to the matter of changing your mentality. One of the very simple things is the type of music you listen to can change the way you think of things, and the personality you have. If you listen to the type of music that is upbeat and positive, you'll most likely perceive the world in that moment in a more constructive and positive attitude. If you listen to music that makes you feel sad or depressed, then you'll have an easier way of perceiving the world in a sad or depressed mood.

Some of the companies that use this to their advantage are film companies. I'm sure you remember those typical teenage movies that always have the same plot and the same begining, middle, and end. They would always start off with the main character sleeping in bed, his alarm clock set to a later time, and then the character realizes they're late for school. The thing that the companies use to their advantage, is the theme song at the beginning. It's always some type of cheery or upbeat song, and whenever the watcher of the movie sees the same scenario playing, with the same type of song, they think to themselves, "Oh, ok, this is another type of regular movie that's always has the same things happening." It might annoy the watcher because they've seen the same thing again and again and again, but they can't help it. They'll have an easier time watching a movie that's the same or similar as other movies they've watched than movies that aren't what they usually watch.

Watchers would rather pay money for a movie that they're familiar with and movies that have the same type of tone, music, and plot, than a movie that has a totally different type of tone, music, and plot than what they usually watch. This can be applied to any other type of business as well. **Make your customers feel like your product is something that they're familiar with. Once you do, you'll not only win their thoughts, but also their emotions.** That's the reason why many businesses around the world make their customers feel like they're at home or make them feel like what they are seeing is something they've seen before. Some of the movies franchises everyone knows always have a similar type of theme song to their movie. Everyone knows the theme songs to Indiana Jones, Marvel, Harry Potter, and Star Wars. When companies use this to their advantage, they win their customers over even if the song's annoying.

Look at Disney and their amusement parks, the whole idea of their amusement parks are about making their customers feel like they've seen what's on the rides, parks, games, and even food. All their rides are themed as a film or movie they've seen before. They never put randomly themed things in their rides. Even their food is themed as a type of character or a type of movie Disney has. It gets to the point that wherever you turn there's always Mickey Mouse looking at you. You turn to the right, Woody the Cowboy is there. You turn to the left, Buzz Lightyear is there. You turn around, Slinky the Dog is there. The point is that companies can easily influence you to buy from them only because they win over your mentality.

You need to have the right mindset in everything you do, whether it be when you're working out, reading a book, or working on your business. That's one of the key things you need to have because it will allow you not only to make your business grow, but to make the right impression on people.

RE-BUILD YOUR PERSONALITY

You might want people to think of you as a "Tony Stark" type of person, or you might want people to think of you as a sweet and caring person, or maybe a serious person that is concentrated on what you're doing, or you might want to make people think of you as funny. Whatever it is, your mentality will help you TREMENDOUSLY. Let's say you want people to recognize you as a confident, good, and bold type of person, then you first have to adjust your mentality to that type of person. Make your mentality and mindset into a smart, confident, and bold type of person while making yourself believe that you are.

Take the action to make you that type of person. Take

a course on charisma, go out and talk to people that you normally don't, get yourself a mirror, and practice talking to yourself like you're the boss - whatever you need to do to make yourself into the type of person you want to be, but remember that it all starts with the mentality of making yourself and believing in yourself, that you're going to become the person you aspire to be. Even if you're a shy person, or someone who doesn't go out much, tell others, like a friend or a family member, to treat you as such. The reason this helps you is because when someone else, besides yourself, acts like you're different or another type of person, it will subconsciously make you believe that you are.

There was an experiment by Stanford University to show that you can be easily influenced, making yourself believe that you're someone different than you usually are just by having others treat you differently. In 1971, Stanford University did the "Stanford Prison Experiment." They took a group of 24 applicants who were mentally and physically healthy, and allowed them to pick if they wanted to be a guard or prisoner. After each of them picked, they were put into a jail cell (basement of the campus) and both the guards and prisoners were told to act like an it was a real prison, and to make the conditions they were in real.

SOURCES:
- https://www.prisonexp.org
- https://www.simplypsychology.org
- https://www.newyorker.com

They were given special numbers just like real prisoners. To make the experience more realistic, the guards were asked to put on mirrored glasses and to avoid eye contact while the prisoners were actually arrested by real life police, put in hand cuffs, and made to put on real prison uniforms with a chain padlock around their legs. The prisoners were to be fed what a real prison would serve, they were told to do pushups--even on each other's backs at times--for a punishment. The only conditions the guards had to follow were to not physically abuse the prisoners.

The experiment was planned to last only two weeks while people were monitoring the prisoners and guards. Then they began. After the first day everything went normally, and both the prisoners and the guards were acting as expected following the rules of not physically abusing the prisoners. However, on only the second day of the experiment the prisoners made a riot wanting to get out of the jail cell. The guards began to make a system that allowed the prisoners to get rewarded and punished depending on what they did just to calm down and manage the prisoners.

After only four days passed, three of the twelve prisoners were traumatized to the point of having to leave the jail cell, saying the conditions were way too real and it was way to disturbing to be treated in such a way. One prisoner, #8612, after 36 hours of being in the cell began to cuss, scream, rant, and yell. The worst part of it was that the observers that were watching each of the guards and prisoners were informed by one of the messengers that he wanted to leave. They easily and quickly said, "You can't leave. You can't quit." Only after they realized that it became serious did they let the prisoners out. The weird thing was that all the prisoners were treated no differently than minimal jail conditions, but not traumatizing.

After a couple more days, the guards themselves became to act ruthless to the prisoners and even to the point of yelling and screaming at the prisoners. It affected the prisoners also; they became depressed and unsettled while still being treated harshly by the guards. At one point a priest came in and offered help to the prisoners. Prisoner #819 broke down and began to cry. On the sixth day, they had to stop the experiment due to the prisoners becoming insane and depressed. It was one of the most recognizable and well-known experiments in the world and a movie about it was released in 2015.

This is obviously a way more serious and dangerous experiment then anyone should attempt, but the concept and idea is there. **Almost anyone can be easily changed physically and mentally by people treating them differently than they usually are, and you can too (for the better).** If you want to be more confident and seem bolder than others, then ask someone close to you to treat you accordingly and put yourself in the environment you would usually be if you were more confident. **This is one of the most valuable things you can learn in this book because you can easily apply it to your life, and it has CRAZY results in only a couple of days.**

In the past years and months there are ways that people prove that with only changing their mentality, they can easily change the way people look at them. How do you think all the icons in sports such as Michael Jordan, Tiger Woods, Serena Williams, Tom Brady, Lionel Messi, Wilma Rudolph, Floyd Mayweather, and many others were able to win so many games and feel fearless? Besides all the hard work and dedication, they always went in to the game with a beast mode attitude. Do you think they went into a game feeling scared and shy? NO, **Whenever the press attacked them with questions they would always answer with confidence, fearlessness, pride, and hunger.**

Whenever the reporters asked them question about the fight or who do they think will win, they'll always respond with "I'm (or their team) always going to win, they (the opponent) are nothing compared to me." Who in a boxing match has ever responded to a reporter and said, "I don't know; I think it's going to be a nice fight. We'll see." They always know that they're going to win the game, no matter what, even if they don't end up winning.

One of the best examples of this is Conor McGregor. He became one of the best UFC fighters in the world and is one of the most respected fighters in the world. Something that always makes his opponents fearful of him is the confidence he has. Whenever McGregor goes up to the ring, he always has the confidence of a lion. When he speaks to the reporters in and out of the ring he always makes everyone around him believe that he will win without a doubt. Of course, all the players say they're going to win the fight and that they'll win the first round or that it'll be a T.K.O. and whatnot, but the thing that separates McGregor from all of the other fighters is the mentality he has in and out of the ring.

Any video you see of him, he always acts like he's the boss and that he owns the room. Even after the fight, he always has his confidence and winning mentality in his mind. He always puts fear into his opponents by either yelling super loud or by a comment he makes, but no matter what, he always keeps the mentality of winning and crushing his opponents in him. He always has confidence in whatever he does, whether it be in a fight or the gym, training.

Even singers and actors have a way to boost their confidence when they're on stage. They never go and perform or act without having the right mentality. Even when I write, I always make sure to be in the right mindset.

Whenever you feel fearful, there's a method you can use to your advantage. It applies in almost any situation where you might doubt yourself or when you're nervous in a public speaking event or in an interview. Almost every athlete does it in a close way. What you do is get yourself in a private room, take a deep breath, and GROWL/YELL AS LOUD AS YOU CAN! This method is called the lion method. Not many athletes and public speakers commonly practice it, but it by far helped me in my past experiences. Some people say you should relax, take your time, and take some deep breaths and in a lot of cases it works for people. However, when you relax and stay still after a couple of seconds, you'll end up, for example, thinking about the fear of fighting again as opposed to winning, when you yell and get all the fear in your body out. This is a very good way to become more fearless than you originally were, or if you just want to become more confident to others and to yourself.

This way is useful in public speaking (more on public speaking in chapter 8). There's no secret when you're doing the lion method, just yell in a room and shake all the fear out of your body. Back to your mentality, **you have to have a hungry, positive, and fearless attitude toward whatever you encounter.** Same with the experiment that I mentioned earlier--if you have a bad attitude toward yourself instead of a positive one, you'll lose.

Remember to use this information with care, as it has some very serious results whether it be good or bad. Use this with care and if you get a chance to share this with someone else, just make sure they don't go crazy.

BEING OPENED MINDED

The last thing you need to change in yourself is **the way you think of things, while always being open-minded on both sides.** First, I want everyone reading this to understand what I mean when I say, "You need to change the way you think of things." What I mean is that when you see things such as arguments, difficult situations, and even in the way you handle your business, don't be locked into one position. Look at all sides. This is one of the biggest lessons to learn, not only in this chapter but in the book.

You'll end up thinking about this whether you want to sell something or create an amazing marketing campaign. What is it? **You have to see both sides of the coin while being open to every opportunity you come across. The reason why viewing both sides of the coin is HUGELY IMPORTANT is because you'll end up encountering more people and opportunities in your life while having more chances of finding the thing you need at the time you need it.**

Being closed minded, and not seeing the importance of viewing both sides of the coin, can easily limit your opportunities of finding what you need, while also limiting the chance of getting what you want. For example, if you're usually an opened-minded person then you should agree with me when I say you become better not only in your life, but also in your business, whenever you see all sides of a situation.

Remember a time in your life when you were arguing with either a friend or family member about a random situation, and got so heated up that you ended up leaving each other? Later that night you clearly see their point of view while feeling terrible about the fight. You could've easily gone without any fight or argument if you had just seen their point of view. Again, it's not easy to just drop the argument and just give it up, but that's what you have to learn to control and master.

A huge example of not only people, but companies, too, being little minded and closed to ideas, is Western Union. Believe it or not, one of biggest giants in companies that deal with money transfers, especially in the 1870's, has made one of the biggest mistakes in history! Although they are still operating, and have a good sum of nine billion dollars in assets, it could've been one of the biggest companies in the world today! In 1876 Alexander Graham Bell offered his patent of the telephone to Western Union for only $100,000. They declined the idea calling idiotic and crazy. Although it was a big blow for Bell, he was determined to commercialize the telephone to everyone around the world.

He went on to found a company that was going to let everyone know about the telephone, and to be their provider. He called it Southwestern Bell Telephone Company, now known as AT&T. A little over a century later they became one of the biggest telephone provider companies in the world competing with Verizon, T-Mobile, Sprint, and so many more with a net worth of over $250 billion dollars! Western Union could've been sitting on a gold mine were they to acquire the patent offered to them by Bell, but no. They were little minded and closed to new ideas back then.

Another company that messed up incredibly bad was Blockbuster when they declined Netflix. This one you might be more familiar with, but for those who are not the gist of it was back in 2000, Netflix co-founders Marc Randolph and Reed Hastings met with the executives of Blockbuster to offer their company (Netflix) to Blockbuster for $50 million. Blockbuster quickly refused the offer calling Netflix laughable and nothing more than a fad. Netflix offered their company multiple times to Blockbuster but their answer was always the same. A couple years later, Netflix became the number one streaming service all over the nation and the world, putting Blockbuster into a position where they no longer had people buying from them until they went bankrupt.

Now, Blockbuster only has one store open in the entire world located in Oregon. Why did blockbuster get kicked out of the game? Because they were too closed to ideas and new opportunities. There are also people that have been opened minded and knew that the future was going to change. Jeff Bezos happens to be the only person in the world that offered to buy Netflix in 1998 for $15 million. Although it was a great offer, Netflix declined saying that Netflix had "more potential," than what was offered.

Just like Northwestern and Blockbuster, Toys R Us found out that they needed to adapt to the future the hard way. In the 1990's they were at their height of success with 1500 stores around the globe and controlling 25 percent of the entire world market! They had it all. Customers, toys, locations, revenue, brand deals, and so much more, which makes it hard to believe everything went from good, to great, to declaring bankruptcy.

On September 18, 2017, Toys R Us declared bankruptcy with over $5 billion in debt. How did they go from being the number one toy store in the world to owing billions of dollars while declaring bankruptcy? Many analysts said that the debt they needed to pay was unbearable for them to pay, but if you do some research on the amount of debt some other companies owe, they surpass the debt Toys R Us had to pay. Look at Netflix; they owe around $14.8 billion which is four times the amount it had in 2016, which was $3.4 billion. So, it couldn't have been all debt that caused Toys R Us to fail.

Another reason analysts say they failed was because of the lack of customers visiting the stores and buying because their original customers from the early 2000's and 90's were already grown up. However, it couldn't have been the lack of customers visiting the store because there's always new kids' being born every year. In addition to having a massive amount of debt and fewer customers, analysts also said it was because they failed to adapt to the new technology being offered to people (online shopping) and that caused them to fail. Yet they did have an online store and a good number of customers shopping there.

So, what caused them to fail? Notice of all three things I listed, they all fall into one thing, lack of leadership. All of the things people said made Toys R Us fail all fall into the lack of leadership. The CEO of Toys R Us in the 90's (Charles Lazarus) saw the future of the company in bad hands because of all of the other competitors in the industry like Amazon. Because of the competition he ended up stepping down from CEO in 1994. In 2005 the company sold itself to Bain Capital and two other partners (Vornado Realty Trust and KKR) for $6 billion which was way less than what they were worth a couple years before. While the first few years was good for the company, and they were doing better than originally, it quickly went wrong, all due to the bad leadership. What can cause leaders to fail? Not being able to change and being unable to see both sides of the coin. In this case, the company itself and the customers.

I can't blame them, they had so many people leaving their store because of other stores that sold the toys cheaper, like Wal-Mart, Target, and Amazon itself. What could they have done instead? Well, you have to keep in mind that kids today want to play physical toys less and less and want to play with their consoles, phones, and PC's more and more. There are things they could've done. They could've gone to the technology game more, they could've marketed themselves as more of a quality brand, they could've expanded more into the global market, or maybe they could've done more of a MAP things (chapter 6).

Whatever they could've done, it was the leaders' (CEO) job to figure it out. Even being the head of the company, it's still hard. You can't just commit to something in an instant. You have to look deep into that idea you have and decide if it's really going to help your company or if it's going to hurt it. Again, that all comes down to being open to new ideas and seeing both sides of the coin being the leaders/CEO's job.

Now that you read of the things that can make you fail when you don't see both sides of the coin, here are the people/companies that have seen the future and made changes for the better. These are the top examples of the things people have done, and the first one is one of the best.

Bob Iger, known as the former CEO of Disney, is one of the best people that have seen the future of people's interest in the movie industry. He became the CEO of Disney in 2005, has grown the company tremendously, and has made Disney multiple world records. He helped Disney grow from having limited films to having multiple revenue streams and companies. What has he done for the company and why was it so successful? One of the earliest things he decided to acquire for Disney was Pixar. What Iger was able to do, which many people can't, is finding out if something is a fad or if it's going to be successful in the long term.

Pixar's CEO at the time was Steve Jobs (RIP). When Bob Iger acquired Pixar from Steve Jobs, Disney's portfolio of movies were many, however the last time they had a huge success was when *The Lion King* came out in 1994. Although Disney at the time was considered one of the best movie companies in the late 90's and early 2000's, they didn't want to lose that title. So, when Bob Iger became CEO, he saw the potential of Pixar and their movies. At that time, Pixar made incredibly good movies, both critically and financially in a row! With movies such as *Toy Story* (1995), *A Bug's Life* (1998), *Toy Story 2* (1999), *Monsters Inc.* (2001), *Finding Nemo* (2003), *The Incredibles* (2004), and many other short films.

When Iger made a deal with Steve Jobs, he planned many more incredible movies. As always there was risk to it. At any moment, if a movie wasn't released, it could have been terrible for both Pixar and Disney, but Iger was right when he acquired Pixar. Instead of failure, they made even more movies with better ratings and more people becoming fans! After a couple of months they started making movies such as *Cars* (2006), which was an incredible success, *Ratatouille* (2007), loved by fans and critics, *WALL*E* (2008),which was loved for the emotional elements, *Up* (2009), which made viewers cry, and *Toy Story 3* (2010), which made a BILLION dollars at the box office, and many other great movies and short films. After much success with Pixar, you don't want to stop there.

Iger went on to acquire Marvel Studios. At that time, Marvel had made a phenomenal success with their movie *Iron Man.* Not only making half a billion dollars at the box office, but the visual effects were amazing while also starting a hero universe. The last movie Marvel made before Disney acquired it was *The Incredible Hulk*. Although not having the same success as *Iron Man* had, it still made a good profit for Marvel with a worldwide grossing of $265 million.

Again, what Iger was great at was figuring out if a studio or movie was a fad or if it was going to be a success in the future. That's something everyone should also learn to master. **People need to figure out if something is going to become a fad (short term) or if it's going to stick with the company or organization for a while.** Facebook did that with Instagram, even though many people doubted them, saying it was going to be a fad and would never become successful. Now look at Instagram and Facbook, they're both in the top 10 best social media apps in the world. **Learn how to identify if something's is going to stick long-term or short-term. Once you do, you'll win both financially and in the way people look at your company.** In Marvel's case, it was definitely not a fad and made Disney the owner of the highest grossing movie in the world, *Avengers Endgame*. With the help of Disney, Marvel made some of the highest grossing movies almost every year.

In 2010, *Iron Man 2* grossed almost $622 million worldwide. In 2011, Marvel made both *Thor* and *Captain America* with a combined total of more than $800 million. Next year they made *The Avengers*, which let everyone know who they were and made$1.5 billion in the box office. In the following years they made some of the highest grossing films in the world and have made Disney and Marvel combined revenue of $22 BILLION. This was a goldmine for Disney, not only financially but also for fans. Everyone and their moms know who Iron Man is, and who The Avengers are. Now Disney is planning to make even more movies with Marvel, whether it is released on the big screen or in digital.

Another success Bob Iger had was with the acquisition of Lucas Films. They're known for making the *Star Wars* and *Indiana Jones* films. Before Lucas Films even thought to sell to Disney, they already made huge movie success, like *Star Wars: A New Hope* with a box office result of $775 million for the first film. *Star Wars: Empire Strikes Back* made$547 million worldwide. The third film in the trilogy, *Star Wars: The Return of The Jedi* grossed$475 million in the box office and many other films that totaled in the billions of dollars.

How can Disney compete with Lucas Films? By buying them. Iger convinced Disney to buy out Lucas Films in order to have the *Star Wars* and the *Indiana Jones* films. They went on to make the films not only better in quality, but also on the financial side. For the *Star Wars* trilogy, Disney made five movies with Lucas Films that have grossed over $5.5 billion. While Disney is planning to make an *Indiana Jones* film in 2022, Iger/Disney have made amazing acquisitions and partnerships through the years, and most of them have worked out.

There are many more things Iger and Disney have

acquired or owned part of in the industry like ABC, an 80 percent stake in ESPN, The History Channel, 67 percent of Hulu, 21st Century Fox, and much more. Marvel Studios, Lucas Films, and Pixar are the most successful companies Disney owns and have made them the most money.

What can you take from Iger and his team? **You have to be opened minded to new ideas and see how things will work. If he didn't see the potential of Pixar, we probably wouldn't have seen some of their greatest movies.** If Iger didn't see what Marvel Studios would become, we would have never seen greatness of the MCU movies and Disney wouldn't have the title having made the highest grossing film on earth. If Disney didn't own Lucas Films, they wouldn't have made one of the biggest movie trilogies in the world, but in the end of the day we do. Why? Because of the CEO's vision for the future and what it would have become, and for seeing both sides of the coin.

Whenever you have the chance to do something good or great for your company, take it. Even if it ends up being bad, do it because the more you try new things and take the chance, you'll be introduced to new opportunities you never had.

Not only Bob Iger has made a company succeed incredibly, but someone who has made a company from scratch and has made it the number one company in its area is Henry Ford. You most likely know who he is and what he's done, so I'm not going to spend too much time on him. For those who don't know or heard of who Henry Ford is, he's the founder of Ford Motor Company. He started in 1903 with 12 investors that invested $28,000 while Ford himself owned 28 percent of the company. Henry Ford launched Ford's first car only a month after founding the company, and the first model was the Model A.

Through the years Henry Ford grew the company, selling 15 million Model T's in 1927. He industrialized cars for everyone and made another big name for people to remember. Although Henry Ford did many things to grow Ford into the number one car company in the world, I want to talk about what he did to make his company different from the others, and what made him wealthy.

At that time (early 1900's), if you saw a car in the street you would you feel amazed! Cars were only for rich people; you would rarely see your friends or family ride in a car unless they had deep pockets. Most options of transportation at that time were railroads, bicycle, horse-drawn carriages, wagons, and, maybe, boats. Although the first car was invented in 1885, they were extremely expensive and difficult to make. It was considered a problem for automakers to make cars easily and sufficiently in mass amounts. Despite the challenge Henry Ford saw in the industry, he knew that cars would soon be available to anyone. He just had to figure out how. After looking any many possible ways to be able to manufacture his cars, he came to the conclusion of making an assembly line of people to make the cars.

The assembly line was a group of people doing one thing only all day to a part of the car. For example, if I were in charge of the tires, I would be near the end of the line only putting tires on the cars, and I wouldn't do anything else. Just putting tires on the cars until my shift was over. That idea of making an assembly line was the best thing since sliced bread! It was affordable, easy to do, consistent, and faster than anything else out there. The great thing that Ford did was to come up with the assembly line while every other manufacture was stuck on only one method, which was slower and expensive. Ford's method cut down the time of making a single car from 12 hours to 2 hours and thirty minutes.

Keep in mind that while he was coming up with things to make his cars be produced faster, many people thought his idea was crazy. How can someone think that owning a car was going to be able to happen in the next couple of years. For all the criticism Ford had, he knew that it was going to be a reality. Why? **Because he was open minded to new ideas and able to see what the future was going to be, a visionary.**

Now let's go from the early 1900's to 1999. A 28-year-old started a company with his friends, called X.com, now known as PayPal. Elon Musk is one of the most influential people in the world today, making huge impacts in space and car travel. You know who he is - everyone does (probably because of memes), and they know what he's done. To sum it all up, he started Zip2, a software company, in 1995 with his brother, Kimbal Musk, and later sold it in 1999. That same year both he and his brother founded X.com, or PayPal, and just like Zip2, they sold X.com for $1.5 billion dollars in stock to eBay. After the success of PayPal, he crated SpaceX hoping to make space flight cheaper and more efficient. Once he founded SpaceX, he invested in Tesla, and later became the majority owner of the company.

Since then, he made Tesla a multibillion dollar auto company and as I'm writing this, it has become more valuable than Ford and General Motors (GM) combined. He's done an incredible job so far, and it's starting to look like he might be the first trillionaire in the world due to asteroid mining. The thing I want to focus on about Musk is what he was able to spot about the future and how he was able to use it to his advantage twice. When he invested in Tesla it could've been the worst thing he had invested in.

In 2004, nobody really knew what an electric car was, besides it wouldn't run on gasoline. It wasn't a common thing to see on the streets. Previous cars that had tried to go electric had failed. So, what could have convinced Musk to invest in Tesla and not another company? Think about it--he could've gone to any other car company. Ford, Volkswagen, GM, Nissan, Chevy, and other companies that showed lasting success. That's the great thing everyone has to learn about Iger, Ford, Musk, Jobs, and so many other like them. They know how to predict the future based on facts and what has happened in the past.

Study Ford--nobody thought that cars would be available in the future and it would just be for the wealthy, but it ended being for everyone. The same thing happened with Musk. Nobody thought that electric cars would go far but they ended up being wrong. Electric cars are now being adopted by many car brands; Tesla, Audi, Volkswagen, BMW, Nissan, and it's going to increase rapidly. It's going to happen again and again and again. Something you need to know that will make you extremely successful is this: **History will always repeat itself. All the successful people know that. Bill Gates did it with Microsoft, Steve Jobs did it with Apple, Elon Musk does it with SpaceX and Tesla, and countless others. Once you know that, you'll be more successful than you ever imagined.**

HABITS

Ok, so you've changed mentally, socially, and in the way you think of things. What else is there to change? Habits. Habits are by far one of the most beneficial and harmful things to have. Think of a habit you have. Brushing your teeth, using your car, seeing your friends, using your phone, eating, etc. As an example, I'll use my phone. I use my phone every day for various purposes. I know since the first day I've had it that I was going to make it a habit to use it. I went from using it time to time, to using it daily, and then, constantly. I did so because of my habits. Not that it was a bad habit. As a matter of fact, I think it helped me a lot, especially in my own companies, but nevertheless it became a habit.

Another example would be my old self in middle school. I would wake up, go to school, and ride my bike home. When I arrived at my house, my grandmother would give me a $10 bill. I would immediately go a local Mexican store and buy three tacos and a big bag of chips. Every day I would do that. Eating tacos again and again. Later, I started to notice I couldn't do as much activity as I used to do because of shortened breaths. I brushed it off thinking I was just growing up and it was natural. I kept on eating tacos and junk food day after day till I got to point of weighing 102 pounds. I was 11 at the time, and a healthy kid at my age would weigh about 80 pounds. I gained 20 more pounds than I originally weighed. It all happened because of one little word--habit.

In this case, my habits ended up making me weigh more than usual, which prevented me from doing things I could've done. That was a bad habit to have. Everyone, including yourself, has habits that either make you better in your life or worse. You need to change the bad habits to good because if you don't, you'll never get where you want to be. Even in your day-to-day life, habits affect you.

No, it's not going to be easy to achieve the habits you want; however it is possible. Charles Duhigg, the author of "The Power of Habits" found the basic but incredible way habits work. In his book he explains that habits work by going about three simple steps. He said, "The first step to a habit is the cue. The cue is anything that triggers your habit, like a certain time or a feeling you may have. For example, if your habit is taking a smoke, your cue would be the craving of the nicotine inside the cigarette. The second part is the routine. The routine is what you do automatically. The routine for smoking is going outside and lighting your cigarette. The third and last part of a habit is the reward. The reward would be the feeling of the nicotine entering your body."

The simplest way to change your habits is clearly define what new habit you want to accomplish. Find a clear and oblivious cue, then define your new routine, and lastly find a strong reward for your habits. Its sounds easier than it is, but at the very least try to make a change in your bad habits.

Another example would be to imagine yourself overweight. On a Sunday night you see the greatest boxing movie of all time, *Rocky*. You go through the whole movie, eating chips and drinking soda, while sitting in your couch. When the movie finished, you get motivated to do something that you've never been able to do, workout. You go to the gym and workout hard and with determination. You do the same thing over and over and over. You start to lose a couple pounds and are feeling better about yourself.

A month goes by and you're doing awesome, but then you miss a couple of days due to work problems. It's fine, you think. Go back to the gym the next time. You go to the gym but the next day you can't go because you committed to your friends to go with them to that special concert you've been talking about. Another day without hitting the gym goes by, but no worries because you say to yourself, "It's only a day right, it's fine to take a couple of rest days." A day goes by, then another and another.

Next thing you know, you haven't worked out in four months and you've gained 55 pounds. WHAT HAPPENED? Habits happened. At the beginning you were going to the gym every day without hesitation, to the point of making it a habit but then you changed because of work, family, friends, etc. You went less and less until you ended up fat and lazy. How can you go back to where you started? Make it a habit again.

First, start by finding your cue. Your new cue might be watching a movie clip from *Creed* or it might be packing your bag the day before. Next, you need to find your routine. Your routine could be going to the gym right after work or maybe you could take a new route to skip all the fast food places on the way to the gym. Lastly, you need your reward. Your reward could be getting a tasty juice to drink after you work out or possibly treating yourself to a little chocolate chip cookie.

You will always have bad habits as well as good ones, but as Charles Duhigg said, **"You can never get rid of your habits, you can only change them into new ones."Try to make as many harmful habits into great habits as you can.**

Change your mentality, your social group, and your habits to be the best you. You don't need to change yourself dramatically, but if you can tell that something or someone is pulling you down instead of making you thrive, then change or leave them.

A huge example of the importance of having habits is a shark and a fish. They both know that they need to swim either away or to each other. They make it a habit because if they don't, they'll both lose. One starves, and one dies, not only in nature, but in the life of billionaires. If you study and look into some of the most successful people in the world, you'll see how habits affect their life in a positive way. They all have similar habits throughout their day that either make them healthier, wealthier, or makes them better in their day-to-day life. Study them, follow them, and apply them. Once you do, you'll have a better chance of being more successful then the other guy next to you.

Oprah Winfrey makes it a habit to eat plenty of vegetables, to be grateful, and get enough sleep (wakes up around 6).She exercises, wakes up early, reads regularly, and makes sure to see her family frequently. Nevertheless, her habits help her both in her life, but also are similar to other billionaires. She became one of the most successful TV show hosts in the world. How did she retire a billionaire? She had many things that made her a billionaire (revenue streams) such as OWN (*Oprah Winfrey Show*) company, Harpo productions, and brand deals. Those are the three main revenue streams that made Oprah the wealthiest TV show host in the world. However, who could she have become if she never applied these habits to her life? If Oprah hadn't applied those habits to her life, she more than likely wouldn't be who she is today. You don't need to copy her exact habits, but make habits of your own that help you both in life and business. Make them daily and nightly habits while making sure you're sticking to them.

Another billionaire that shares similar habits as Oprah is Mark Zuckerberg. The co-founder of Facebook is in the top 10 wealthiest people in the world. What are his daily habits and routines? He wakes up at 8:00 in the morning, and immediately after he wakes up, he looks at his phone and checks on Facebook, Whatsapp, Facebook Messenger, and does any other task he can do from his phone. Like Oprah, they both work out daily, with Zuckerberg making sure he runs at least three times a week.Still, he hits the gym daily. He makes sure his family is always a priority, and he makes sure to see his wife and children every day. I want you to notice that everything he does, from waking up early to seeing his family everyday, he always makes it a habit to do those things.

Do you see the similarities between him and Oprah? They both wake up early; make it a priority to exercise every day, both of them see their family daily or as much as they can, and they both are billionaires.

Alexander Jimenez (yes, that's me!) is another soon-to-be-billionaire that has the same or similar habits other billionaires have. He wakes up at four in the morning, making sure he has some time to himself, and works out around 30 minutes after he wakes up. He runs almost every day while trying to make sure he gets a good 1-2 hours of exercise in.

While reading regularly, he also makes it a habit to learn new business things he doesn't know, or things he doesn't know much of. He either works in his company SAC (Smiles Against Cancer), or works on his upcoming book. Just like other billionaires, he makes sure to see all of his family daily or at least call them. Something to take in is that Jimenez has the similar habits and routines of billionaires.

Not only Oprah, Zuckerburg, and Jimenez, but almost all billionaires have the same habits. Bill gates wakes up early in the morning regularly and goes on the treadmill, Jeff Bezos starts his day with important meetings and spends time with his family whenever he can, and Richard Branson wakes up at 5a.m., and makes sure he's health is great. Again, you don't need to copy their exact habits, but whenever you can, try to apply the same notion as them.

If you have free time, go and work on your company, read, work out, etc. Try to wake up early and get that free time in your day dedicated to your family. Remember the more habits and routines you copy from someone you admire, you're more likely to become similar to that person.

Want to be closer to a billionaire? Then follow the steps and habits billionaires do. If you want to become a professional basketball player, then follow the same habits, steps, and routines that other players do. The same goes for any type of career. **Whoever you want to become, you'll have a higher chance of becoming that person if you follow the habits and steps a person like that would usually do.**

Before you go on to the next chapter, remember that although you're taking in great information, you need to take the action to apply it to your life, and make sure to use it, not just say that you've read this. Remember, you can learn everything you need to learn about business, a sport, writing, etc., but if you don't take the action to apply it to your life or in the situation you need it in, then it's a waste of time. Remember, you've got this!

CHAPTER TWO

ESCAPE THE WORKER MINDSET

"You don't have to be a genius or a visionary or even a college graduate to be successful. You just need a framework and a dream."

~Michael Dell

———————

RAT RACE

YES! It's finally the weekend! It's time to relax, party, and have fun. The weekend goes by fast, until you come to a realization that Monday's coming up and it's time to work again. You go through the week working in a little cubical or if you're in school, working at little wooden desks, and you want to go home, but it's not time yet. After your day is done, you come home tired and frustrated that your new boss is the worst thing that happened to you. You do the same routine every day while feeling like you could do something else, something better than what you're doing currently. Years pass and you start to think of retirement. You keep working over and over and over again, until you realize that you're in a retirement home. You start to regret not taking your chance with that girl, not starting your dream business, or not going on that special vacation you've always dreamed of.

So many regrets, but by the time you notice you should've done this or done that it's already too late. You're old and tired all the time, but you can't do anything about it. Time passes and then out of nowhere you start to feel dizzy, your heart starts to pump faster and faster, and you don't know what's happing. But then...you see a bright light. You've died. This is the life of millions of people around the world that were brainwashed to think that's the way to live your best life.

Alright, I might have exaggerated a bit, but that's a

harsher way of saying it. However, it's the same notion and idea. Think of your early days of middle school or even high school, you've been told by society and teachers that working for someone and having a regular job was accepted by society and that's what you need to be happy in life.

On the other hand, having the passion to make a business yourself, dropping out of school, or being an entrepreneur was considered a risk and the acceptance of failure. If you were to start a business in the 80s, 90s, or early 2000s, you were considered weird or in other words, an outcast. You would've been dealing with criticism, haters, discouragement, and disliking of others if you were to start a business at that time. Despite all of that, we're now in a new era that makes it easier, and even supports starting a business.

The whole idea of working a typical 9-5 job, going to college for years, just to get a degree, owning a house with a spouse and a couple kids, and anything else in the "American Dream" is called the *Rat Race*. It was introduced to the world by Robert Kiyosaki in his book "Rich Dad Poor Dad." An overview on what makes a person stuck into the rat race is when **"Employees work harder to get a promotion by their employer/boss, and how even though they make more money in their paycheck, they end up increasing their spending habits while not investing into assets, but into liabilities.** They go on this self-defeatist cycle that keeps on going again and again and again." Rich Dad Poor Dad is a great book for all beginners who want to go more in depth into the middle-class mindset and the rat race.

We're not only fortunate, but extremely lucky, to live in a time where society is becoming more welcoming to the idea of entrepreneurship and of not needing a degree to be successful in life. You can now share your opinion or idea to everyone in the world without the need to pay for your idea to be heard. Furthermore, it's the reason why people now are able to understand others that say, "Completing the 17 years of your school life is not necessary to get a job and to be happy in your personal life," even to the point where it's starting to become more popular to become an entrepreneur.

As a result, you, as well as anyone in the world, can easily create a company that could be based on whatever you want. You can even make whatever passion you have into a business. If you're in love with the game *Call of Duty* (COD), you can make it into a business by selling COD based products, making a podcast about COD, or anything else in the world. Of course it's not as easy as just saying you going to create a business, you want it to actually make revenue and become a real company, not just a hobby. It's so much easier to not only create a business in general, but one that's based on what you like than it was years go.

There are things people need to understand before starting a business, which is the reason almost 50 percent of businesses fail in their first five years. Although creating a business is now being accepted more than ever, and more and more people are considering business owners cool, it's not an easy job. You're going to encounter countless failures, milestones, challenges, and in many cases, go broke.

That's the reality of it. Many people go into business at random and don't know where they're going, just thinking that they'll figure it out as they go. That's the ABSOLUTE WORST thing you could do. That's why many people fail when they start a business--they don't look at what's actually happening and what they are getting into, because instead of making sure that they know that will be struggles in front of them, they just forget about them and decide to start it anyway. Not only the fact that people forget that there are challenges financially and physically, but it's also a great risk to start a business in many ways.

As I'm writing this, the entire world's economy is on the brink of collapsing and many small business are shut down due to social distancing. In many cases their business is their only source of income and they have bills to pay. They need to put food on the table, they still have to pay rent, and, if they have a family to take care of, its going to be way worse for them than people who don't.

Think of yourself in that same scenario, you take out your life savings and you have an idea for a business that you think will be the next Amazon. You start it while believing you're going to succeed no matter what. Everything's going your way until BAM; a virus just hit China and it's going overseas. Next thing you know, people are going crazy, buying all the toilet paper and everything's getting shut down. If you put in everything you had into that business and almost nobody can buy your product or service because the government isn't letting you sell due to social distancing, what are you going to do for money? In the case that you have money saved up, which might not be much because you spent all your money in that business, it's not going to last long. On top of that, almost all companies are being shut down, so you're not going to be able to get a job. What are you going to do? You might think I'm exaggerating but that's the harsh reality, especially now, in the time we're in, the Covid-19 pandemic of 2020.

Here's some messed up math for you. The average family income in America is $75,000. I want to remind you that is how much an average American makes from their job, surveys, raffles, etc., combined. So, when someone makes $75,000, it's not all from their job. Anyway, let's dig deep into their expenses and how much they're really left with after all the deductions.

An average American spends shy of $7,500 on food, around $2,000 a year on gas, $3,000 year dedicated for entertainment purposes (movie theaters, shows, TV, streaming services, etc.), just below $1,500 each year on education, care products and services cost them $800, clothing costs them $2,000 a year (including watches, shoes, sweatshirts, etc.), $4,000 a year on car repairs, healthcare takes away another $5,000 a year, $7,000 per year for personal insurance, $14,000 a year goes to their child's needs and wants, to organizations and charities they donate $2,000, and, to top it all off, an average American pays just below $20,000 a year for mortgage/housing. $68,800 is what a median income in America pays in total! What does that leave them with? Only $6,200 is left after all the expenses and deductions.

Although, to many people, having over $6,000 to spend freely on what I want seems great, but that's before taxes. The top one percent of taxpayers pays 26.76 percent in taxes; the other 99 percent pay 11.4 percent on taxes. Let's be safe and go for the middle, assuming 15.36 percent is what the average American pays in taxes. 15.36% of $68,800 is $10,444! So, in reality, if you're an average American you'll be in debt a little over $4,000. Not so great now, right?

In a lot of cases the end figure is going to change, taking into consideration that some people make more or less than $75,000 a year.However, that's the base price for the average person in the US. I don't want to make it seem like being in the middle-class group in America is bad; I'm just saying that the "American Dream" isn't as dreamlike as you might think, especially if you're born and raised in America.

For those that are still happy with the idea of starting a business, and not knowing the challenges you're going to have, let's just pretend that the economy is normal and nothing crazy's going on in the world. For example, let's say that you're starting a grocery store. Let's list some things you're going to have to do. For one you're going to have to work all day restocking your products whether it be online or a physical store. Unless you have a personal assistant that's good with numbers, you're going to need to learn accounting. If you're bad in accounting, you're pretty much going to get lost in the numbers side of the business, and you have to make sure that the store or website is in good condition, looks professional or whatever way you want it to be, that you can pay the rent (if it's a physical store) month after month, and so many more things you need to consider.

I honestly don't want to scare you, or take away the chance of you starting a business, but I want to make sure you know what you're going to face. Having and creating a business is awesome and fun, but there's also another side to it, which I don't think people are talking about. It's getting easier to create a business year after year and doesn't need to be risky, but you always having to be prepared for what's coming.

Moreover, when your company starts to get bigger the challenges are also going to get bigger. More customers require more inventory, and more success also breeds more challenges, and the more you win, the more haters you're going to have. At the end of the day, business is the "job" that can make you wealthier than any other job or occupation, but it's also one of the hardest ones to learn. Just make sure you know what you're getting into, and if you're 100 percent sure that you're going to start a business, then get ready for a rollercoaster of things.

ASSETS & LIABILITIES

One of the most important things you need to know in order to become extremely successful in financial wealth or what makes you part of the rat race is the difference between assets and liabilities. They're what makes or breaks your financial wealth. Think of assets and liabilities as a literal gold mine.

What do gold mines need to operate? They need the tools, the carts, drills, the location, the railing, etc. So, an asset is the drills, carts, pickaxes, and anything else that helps you get to the gold. On the other side of the coin, liabilities are anything that takes away the chance of you getting closer the gold such as the other side of the mine (where you take away the gold), rain, storms, dull tools, problems with the tools, a blocked entrance, etc. The difference between the tools and the problems is that one helps you get the gold (money) and the other makes you spend money, like the sharpening of the tools, getting the money to drain the rainwater away, and anything else that made you spend money that wasn't a need.

The easiest way to say it is, assets are what you should

always have and **assets are anything that gives you money. Some examples of assets are profitable stocks, bonds, real estate, companies, properties, antiques, and anything that can put money into your pocket rather than taking money away. The other ones are the liabilities: liabilities are anything that takes money away from you such as an unneeded car, your house, going to eat at your favorite fast food place, new clothes, partying, wasting money with your friend, and anything that takes money out of your pocket.** Assets are one of the first things people fail to master, which in turn makes them not only less wealthy, but makes them need a regular job, which in many cases they hate because of the time, leadership, pay, etc.

It sounds simple enough right? All I have to do to create financial wealth is to buy things that make me money all the time and not spend my money on things that decrease my wealth. Yes, that's pretty much it, but it's not that easy. It's not so easy to get someone to spend their money, and at times it could be all they have. I want you to think of something that you want badly, not "I kinda want it," but if I could pick this or anything else in the world I would pick IT. It could be a new pair of Yeezys, a new iPhone, an Xbox, a pair of movie theater tickets, a place or school you want to move to, etc.

Whatever that thing is will be Option A. The next option you have is Option B. The value in this option could be great or it could be worth nothing, nevertheless this is what it is. Option B is a stock option of a nano technology company worth around $15 a share. There's nothing special about it, just a normal startup company that is on its way to make nano tech accessible to everyone.

Think about it, you have the most desired thing you want in one hand and a stock option available to you in the other. Which would you pick? If you picked something that is truly significant to you it's going to be a hard choice. So, what would you pick, if you've read everything in this book so far you probably have the stock choice in your head right now? Well whichever option you picked it's important to note that it was a difficult choice.

That's what makes it hard to have assets over liabilities. If you have the money on hand and you have the option to pick either something that will make you money or something that you want, you're most likely going to pick that desired thing you want. You might be saying to yourself that if you were given the option yourself you would pick the asset instead, right? Although you might say that to yourself now, your brain is going to change thoughts if you were to be put on the spot.

Another Stanford University experiment--it's not going to be as harsh as the first one in chapter one. This one is light-hearted but still show's that you can easily be influenced, not by social connections like the first one, but by temptation. You might have know or heard of this one, the "Stanford Marshmallow Experiment". The basics of it included a group of children that were placed into a private room, one at a time, with a marshmallow. A man came into the room and told them that he was going to leave the room and if they didn't eat the marshmallow they would be able to get two. When the man left the room, the researchers found various results. Some kids ate the marshmallow immediately after the man left, some kids waiting a bit until they had to dig in, others went on to last around 10 minutes until they couldn't resist the urge, and some kids waited the full length of time until the researcher came back. After the test was over, and after they got their results, they went on to wait a couple of years for the kids to graduate a grade in school. When they came back to see how and what the kids had done in that period of time (until freshman year) and to see what their grades were, the results blew their minds!

The kids that resisted the urge of eating the marshmallow until the researcher came back in the room got higher SAT scores than the other kids that ate the marshmallow before he came back. After they did even more research, they found out that although the kids that ate the marshmallow before the man came back got lower scores than the kids who didn't, they still ranked higher on their SAT's the longer they resisted the urge to eat the marshmallow. Basically, what they found out was that kids had a higher chance of getting a higher SAT score than another kid who took less time to eat the marshmallow than them.

How does this correlate to assets and liabilities? The way people think of assets and liabilities is the same way the kids thought of the marshmallows. **People tend to want rewards fast rather than waiting a little bit longer to get a better reward. That's the thing that keeps people from acquiring assets--in order to make money in big quantities by utilizing assets, it typically takes longer than people are willing to wait.**

What's the first thing that comes to mind when someone asks "what is the typical way to make a lot of money, besides owning a business?" Stocks. That's why stocks are considered one of the biggest assets to have in order to make money. They're considered the best thing to have, even if you work in a job. For the vast majority of people, their way of buying and owning assets are their 401k. That's the only asset they have besides their job. By the way, a 401k plan doesn't make you much money, even in the long term, and most of the money they take from the paycheck to "invest" in is 90 percent of their own company.

Assets take time to compound, unlike liabilities which you can get in one swipe of a card. **Assets for the most part are things that need time to compound to a lot of money.** The reason that I say assets take time to create wealth is because most of the assets people know of are the ones that take time. **Instead, go and find assets and things that can**

make you money short and long-term. Don't wait for the gold to find you--go out and find it. An example of an asset that happens to take quite a bit of time to make money is stocks. I mentioned that stocks are the first thing that comes to mind when people think of assets because they take time to make money and much studying of them which also takes a long time. But that's only one of hundreds if not thousands of assets you can have.

So, what are the most reliable and wealth creating assets to have? There are three assets that **allow you** to create massive amounts of wealth. Although these three assets have a higher chance of creating more wealth then say most other assets; make sure you take the words "allow you" in a serious way. Yes, these assets make you a lot of money and wealth, but they can easily make you lose almost all of your money or a significant amount if you don't know what you're doing.

Educate yourself in each of these subjects before you start to invest in them. When you invest into these assets, they create a higher chance of risk of losing your money than if you didn't invest in them, but you always have the ability to control the risk. That's the reason you need to educate yourself into each of these subjects so you know exactly what you're doing. Although it's pretty obvious that you need to learn these subjects before you begin to put money into them there are a lot of people who have no idea what they're getting into.

In 2008, one of the biggest recessions in American history happened with the value of houses dramatically decreasing, and on top of that, the stock market crashed. As a result, over 11 million people lost their jobs, lost their house, had no money for basic essentials, and so many people suffered. Millions started getting loans from banks and buying houses without making sure that what they were putting their money into was a secure asset, or at least they could pay the debt back. Before September 2008 (the month the recession happened) everyone was having a jolly good time buying things they didn't need and buying houses, not because they had the money, but because they had the chance to buy the banks. Instead of doing their "homework" on what they were doing and why the banks were lending them huge amounts of money--not thinking "is there something wrong here" they ignored the thought and just went for it. A couple months later they had thousands of dollars in debt while a recession was happening. The recession of 2008 is difficult, and if you want to go more in depth into what caused it you can find a video on it on YouTube.

Anyway, the point of this is that although these three assets are the most powerful and wealth creating ones, **you need to educate yourself on them before you think about investing in them. Make sure you know exactly what you're getting into and how to manage the risk of losing your initial investment in anything you're doing.**

Enough lectures, let's get into it. **The top three assets that make you the most money than any other assets are real estate, business, and stocks.** These are the most powerful assets to get into and allow you to create millions and billions of dollars. Although it might seem obvious that these are the top three assets, what most people don't understand is how to work them and they're scared to invest in them because of the risk. Well, why real estate, business, and stocks?

Let's dig into the first asset, real estate. Real estate is one of the only assets that you can see, touch, smell, breathe, or, in other words, it's a tangible asset. Real estate is the best asset for people who want a secure, tangible, and stationary asset. Unlike stocks and a business, you can physically touch real estate and make sure it's always there.

This asset is for people that want something more on the secure side, and for people that want something that doesn't decrease and increase in value every day. If you want to invest into real estate, the top people you're going to want to look into are Tom Ferry (founder of Ferry International), Ryan Serhant (sold over 170 million dollars of real estate in 2019 only), Barbra Corcoran (founder of The Corcoran Group and part of the show *Shark Tank*), and Grant Cardone (CEO of Cardone Capital which has over a billion dollars in real estate). They're the some of the top real estate experts and many of them have courses, YouTube videos, and books that you can educate yourself with. If you're thinking of investing in real estate, that's great, just make sure you know what you're doing.

The next asset is having a business. It's the most basic, but one of the most powerful assets to invest in. The great thing about owning a business is that practically anyone can have one while having the opportunity to work from home. Unlike stocks and real estate, you can create a business without needing any startup money in some cases. It's a great asset to have/operate for all people. For stay-at-home parents or people who have extra time in their day, having a business could be a side job that can create extra money for the month. However, having a business is also for people who want to seriously create massive amounts of wealth. If you dedicate yourself to creating and growing your business, you'll have a higher chance of "making it" than the guy next to you. Just like real estate and stocks, owning your company always has risk. Not that it's a bad thing, because almost every asset has some risk whether it's low or high but you have to learn how to manage it.

The great thing about business that other assets don't have is that you can manage the risk of your business better and easier than say the other two assets. In real estate you can't really change the value of the property unless people are in the market for it or if you add things to it to make it seem more appealing. The same thing goes for stocks— unless you're the owner of the company, you can't really know if the stock value is going to increase or decrease. It's not a gamble, in any case, but it's not as easy to change the value of it as having a business. The biggest advantage of having a business over the other two assets, is that you can physically change the value and risk of the company. Although business is harder to manage than the other two assets, owning a business is one of the best ways to create massive wealth.

Last but not least, stocks. Stocks are one of the top three assets to have, but if you learn how to master it you'll be able to make more money than both in business and real estate combined. To clarify, when I say stocks are one of the best assets to invest in, I'm saying stocks, bonds, options, and foreign exchange, in general. The reason stocks are the #1 asset to have that makes you money--both long and short term--is because stocks allow you to buy part of every other asset of the top three. If you're not interested in owning and operating a business, but you still want to make profit from one, then you can invest in one by owning stock of a company. If you're not interested in owning or working real estate property you can invest into a real estate company.

The advantage of stocks that both having a business and real estate don't, is that stocks allow you to invest into companies without being involved or part of that company directly. I'm not saying that you never have to worry about the stocks you own. What I'm saying is that unlike having a business, you don't need to be part of the company directly.

The same with real estate, you don't need to own real estate directly to be part of it. With stocks you can be practically part of any company, business, or organization without working for them (as long as they're publicly traded).

The only "downside" to stocks is that although they make you the most money, they require more education than real estate and business combined. Unless you're going to own stocks as a hobby or not taking it seriously, then you're going to need to study and educate yourself on stocks a lot. Although learning stocks is not rocket science, it's harder than your average school test. I don't want to take anything away from stocks, but I want to make it clear that before you get into the market it's going to be a lot prettier if you do your homework first.

Before I get any farther into this chapter, and into the pros and cons of each asset, I want to tell you a little acronym that once applied to whatever career you'll to end up getting you'll have an easier time getting more wealth and time than you ever imagined.

Availability of Earth (AOE). What AOE means is whatever job or business you have, you're going to have the availability to work from anywhere in the world, or in this case the earth. AOE allows you to have more time and wealth. The reason it allows you to have more wealth is because almost every asset I told you of (real estate, stocks, and business) allows you to work from anywhere on planet Earth, AOE. Real estate is everywhere on earth (in countries cities, towns). Same with owning a business--you can do business almost anywhere on earth (gold mines, international manufacturing, your company building). Stocks allow you to work anywhere on earth (with internet) by trading on companies around the world, foreign exchange, etc. All of these three assets can create you HUGE amounts of wealth by working anywhere on earth.

Although some assets have more flexibility than others, and some need you to be there more often than a regular job, you still can make your own hours and time without someone telling you where or when you need to come in. AOE is open to more than just the three I mentioned, such as artists, singers, athletes, public speakers, etc. because those jobs also allow you to work around the world. However, the top three assets/ careers (real estate, stocks, and business) make you more money than any other job and asset. Once you apply AOE to any job and career you have, you'll then be able to have the freedom of time and wealth.

I'm going to list both the pros and cons of each of the three assets, but I don't want to seem like I'm taking away anything from it. They're still the top three assets to have so don't think that any one of them is worse than I initially said it was.

REAL ESTATE	STOCKS	BUSINESSES
-Appreciation over time -Asset/investment that everyone needs at all-time -You're operating it, unlike having a stock in the company where you have no say in what the company does	-You can have part of any publically traded company/ market -You have more options to make money both long and short term -You can profit overtime no matter what condition the world's economy is (people are currently profiting in the medical industry)	-You have a say in what happens to the business (AKA - you're in control of what happen to the business unlike stocks) -You can make partnerships, transactions and sales all over the world unlike stocks where you can only trade in the US market (unless you trade in the Foreign Exchange market) -You can sell an actual product or service

I want to quickly mention that the graph above this shows both the pros and cons of each asset. They're all great in their own way, and they all have their own edge that others don't, but none of them are the best one to have in every situation. The reason for this graph is to show you which asset is the best to focus on in your situation. For some people they don't have as much time as others so they might pick business and stocks over real estate. For others, they might have the time but not the money so in their case they would pick business over the other two. Figure out which asset is the best to have in your situation, then take action to get it.

So, you know what the top three assets are to have--how about the other ones? Well, here are some honorable mentions. Gold or any other type of material. It's a great asset because gold rarely decreases in value over time; treat it as a bank. Collectibles items--sport cards, sports memorabilia, game cards, and any type of collector's edition item. Treat collectibles as an asset that increases in value over time and hold onto it until it becomes more valuable than what you originally paid for it. Antiques are other great assets to have. Such as paintings, old technology, statues of all sizes, sculptures, etc. Treat them like a collectible; it's an item that increases over time. It also is something someone could be looking for that only you have. There are countless assets that are available. I can't list all in a chapter, much less a paragraph, but the ones I mentioned wraps up most of them.

The top three assets by themselves can make you massive amounts of money. All of them can make you a billionaire if you dedicate yourself to them. However, the best advice I can give you on the subject of assets and liabilities is this. **All assets are great to acquire; however, why not have as many assets as possible? Whether it be gold, real estate, stocks, businesses, collectibles, or antiques, if you have the ability to get as many assets as you can, why not go for all of them?**

The last thing I want to leave you with before you head on into the next subject is one asset that is more valuable than any other asset in the world combined. Everyone has this asset, but almost everyone takes it for granted until it's too late. Unlike any other asset, we can lose this one in a snap of a finger.

This asset is time. **Time is the most valuable asset everyone has, but the one everyone takes for granted. You can have all the money, cars, houses, and anything you want in the world, but if you lose your time on this earth, you won't be able to use any of it.** You, me, our neighbor, friends, family, and everyone on earth doesn't know when their last time on earth will be. Although this book has wisdom that you can use to make your dreams come true, none of it will be worth it without you being alive. **Time is so valuable, but so limited in our life. We never know when we will be gone and dead. Can you manage it or make more of it? Well, yes and no. You can't guarantee how long you will live, but you can at least try to extend it.**

That's the reason having wealth is important. With wealth, you can pay a doctor to cure a disease you could have. If you have wealth, you can pay someone to take care of you if you can't care for yourself. With wealth, you can make the most of your time on this earth by paying for something you want. Do you want to go skydiving, bungee jumping, own a new car, pay for healthcare, buy a big house, be comfortable in whatever way suits you? Well, with wealth you can. Time is the most important thing we have; make the most of it and be happy in it. Live life the way you want to. Although it's going to take some time, it's possible.

WHY DON'T OTHERS START A BUSINESS?

There was a quote by Robert Kiyosaki that not only makes perfect sense, but captures the exact meaning of why working for someone else is one of the biggest contributing factors that makes people fall into the rat race. He said, "They (referring to an average worker) get up every day and go work for money, not taking the time to ask the question, 'Is there another way?'" The reason this is one of the best quotes that describes people who are stuck in the rat race is because **although many people admit to hating their job, or feeling they can't do something else, they only know one way to make money, which is by working for someone else.**

No, not all people hate their jobs or feel like they want something more. Many people feel fine with what they have, and that's great for them. They might just want a good house with a good paying job and they're happy with what they have. Not everyone wants a huge house or to live with the stress of running a company, and that's what makes them happy. However, what the majority of people want is to be living with the greats, and to have it all.

Think about yourself, what would you pick? Obviously, they're both a bit different from the core truth of it and some require more work than others in certain area's, but the idea is the same. Choice #1, a medium-income job, living in a good neighborhood, one or two vacations a year, having a good time with your friends on the weekends drinking beer, and having a good husband or wife, possibly kids. Or, Choice #2, having to work for yourself, getting paid very well, living in a mansion, going wherever you want to go, not needing to think about the money, you just go wherever you want, being surrounded with people who can help you in creating more wealth and to grow your business, and doing all of that with your family.

I'm guessing that you picked Choice #2 as many others probably would, but whichever one you picked, something they both have in common is that they're both possible. Although they both require work in areas, and one more than the other, they both can become possible if you're willing to put in the work.

On one side you need to be willing to work years of your life dedicated to school education, you need to make sure you find a secure job that pays well, you need to make sure you show up to work every day, etc. On the other side you need to make sure you're willing to live poorly for a couple years of your life, you need to put years into financial and business education, you're going to want to find a mentor or some way to learn from someone directly from the source (better than Google), willing to not hang out with your typical friends, and to put yourself in better friend groups, etc. Before we go any deeper, I want you to know that a lot of things that are in the next part of this chapter are most likely going to contradict past things your parents might have told you, so unless you already know what to expect, try to have an open mind to everything you read.

I want to share a true story with you that shows how challenging and the harsh the truth about starting your business can be, especially in the beginning. In the streets of San Francisco there was a man (we'll call him Chris) with a toddler and an unsupportive wife in the 1990s to early 2,000's. Chris never grew up rich or with a lot of money, so he came to adulthood from almost nothing. After college both he and his wife bought a small apartment, with him working as a lab assistant. The job paid only $8,000 a year, which wasn't even close enough to pay for basic necessities like food, mortgage, car, etc. Although everything was going smoothly, his wife got pregnant and now they would have another mouth to feed.

A few years later he was unable to provide for his family. He sold bone density scanners (a slightly better X-ray) for doctors that almost no one wanted. Not being able to take care of himself and his family, he got hit with a huge blow- -his wife left him and his son. After getting kicked out of his apartment, he and his four-year-old son had to move to a smaller apartment and because he had no car, asked a friend to help.

However, one day he heard of a training seminar in a brokerage house located in Wall Street that would last months for the position of being a real broker. He decided to apply for the job, not knowing if he would get accepted. Once all the applicants went for the job, only a couple of them got the chance to be a real broker. The man was accepted.

The job didn't pay him, so he had to drop his son off at a local daycare every day while selling his bone density scanner to doctors and going to the training seminar all at once. Months went by with him and his son living in poor conditions on the bare minimum a person could. After selling a good amount of density scanners he was able to pay for both food and his house, and was able to live a bit better. Everything was going his way when another hit right to the face came as he was unable to pay his taxes and the only scanner he had was broken.

As a result, he got kicked out of his apartment with nowhere for he and his son to go. In the middle of the night he had to find shelter for them. They were forced to go in a subway station with only the luggage they could carry, and no food or money.

Before I go any further into the story, I want you to put yourself in the same position. You and your child just got kicked out of your apartment, your wife left you, you have no money and are forced to go to a subway station, and, on top of all of that, you're left with only one thing to provide for money; a broken scanner that you only have one of. What are you going to do? All of your possessions and valuables are stripped away in a snap. Think about that.

Anyway, back to the story. The man is left with nothing except a broken machine which is the only way to provide for both him and his son. What does he do? He keeps on going; trying to fix his broken machine, attending the sales program, caring for his son, and suffering in the process. However, there's always a silver lining if you keep working for your dream. In the following months of agony, the man comes to the test and the results of his work in the brokerage house.

At this point he feels defeated, both as a dad and an entrepreneur. He packs his bags for what he thinks is the end of his time at the brokerage house, worried he failed the test. As he gets ready for the end of his day and work, he gets called out by the decision makers and heads of the program. Getting ready for his dismissal, he sits down and gets ready for the news. The men asked him various questions--what have you experienced in your time at the program, how do you think you scored in the test compared to the others, what would you do if you passed the test and become a certified broker? As the man gets bombarded with questions, he thinks to himself, "Could this be? Did I get the job?" Time passes until Chris tells the men, "I thought I'd wear a nice shirt today, being the last day and all." One of the men speaks up and tells Chris, "Thank you, we appreciate that. But wear one tomorrow, too, ok? Because tomorrow's going to be your first day, if you'd like to work here as a broker."

BAM! Crazy ending, right? After the months of agony and terrible conditions of Chris's life, he untimely gets the job! The man in this story is Chris Gardener. Gardner is now a speaker and businessman. After becoming one of the most successful people in the brokerage house, he founded his own brokerage firm, Gardener, Rich & Co. in 1987. Gardener is now one of the few people that have a movie made about their personal story.

The movie name is "The Pursuit of Happiness" and Chris is played by Will Smith. His book is also named, "The Pursuit of Happiness." Although you probably saw the ending to this story, I want you to think about this and find out what the golden nugget is. **The reason people decide to shy away and forget the idea of starting their own business is because they find out that it's not all "rat race lifestyle to living in their dream life." Although people might want to start their business and end up creating one, sooner or later they're going to encounter the struggles of it. They don't want to face the reality that they might live to be in Chris' shoes if they depend solely on their business.**

Yes, this is the typical things you hear from almost all the guru's and the Tony Robbins of the world. But, please, sink this into your brain for a minute. If you start your business and decide to go all into it, you legitimately can end up homeless and needing money if you don't have anything to lean on and you end up failing. But that's what all the people trying to sell you courses, lectures, seminars, and anything that they make you believe is helpful, don't tell you. At the least a good portion of them.

At the end of the day, what I want you to understand about starting your business is this. **Be prepared to fail. Be prepared to end up losing almost all the time at the start. Be prepared to encounter haters, followers, and critics. Be prepared to live in bad conditions if you don't have the good start. But always remember this quote by Denzel Washington whenever you fail or are at the brink of failing. *"Fall Forward."*** Although this quote is short, it's one of the biggest things to remember when you're starting out. ***"Fall Forward"*** means to learn from what you failed at whether it be something small or something big. When you fail, learn, accept, overcome, heal, and bounce back from your failure. Own your mistakes while finding the errors of them. When you truly accept this, you'll become invincible to the fears of failures and mistakes.

Before you get on the next part of the chapter, I want to leave you with this. The worker mindset is a huge killer for dreams. Every day around the world there are millions of dreams people have that could be revolutionary for mankind. It could be anything from making a new type of dish soap to building a nano technology company but every day people's dreams get crushed and shut down due to their boss, friends, family, teacher, or comrades telling them "You must be OUT OF YOUR MIND for thinking that will work" or "That's crazy, you'll only make your life worse" and maybe, "Be quiet and just do your homework. That won't put food on the table."

Yes, you will encounter people like that all the time,

but just keep on going. Of course, it's not as easy as that and it will never be, but if you focus on the haters 24/7, your mentality will go from "YES, I CAN DO THIS" to "Maybe I was just kidding myself and my million dollar idea is just a dream."

WHO'S DONE IT, EXAMPLES

You might have heard of Tony Robbins. One of the greatest motivational speakers in business, and in life. People pay thousands of dollars just to speak with him one-on-one for only an hour. He's worth over half a billion dollars and lives an amazing life in Fiji with his wife Saga Robbins.

What people might not know about him is that he was originally a janitor and only got paid $40 each week! Think of yourself as him at the time he was a janitor. Would you give up on your life, and quit a 9-5 cleaning job that pays $40 a week? I'm betting that a handful of people would. Not Anthony Robbins. He kept on working but also learning about business and entrepreneurs. He went to seminars and talks with all the money he had. In the end, he became one of the biggest giants in talks about life and business.

There was a big chance he could've been another daily Joe in society working for a boss while being told what to do but, no, he kept on pursing his dreams, to become what he is today while saying no to the working class society. After years of embarrassment he slowly but surely started to become more and more successful. And now look at him. He's now known as one of the most successful people in the world having millions of followers that both listen and come to his seminars around the world, while having many bestselling books and audiotapes.

Another self-made successful millionaire is Jim Carrey. Although he's now known as one of the best actors ever in comedy, and in general, he also had a bad start in his career. He lived in his car for a big part of his life. Not only did he live in his car, but he didn't get much work, and he needed to provide for himself. Everyday without a job meant he didn't know if he was going to eat or not. After years of living in his car and struggling to find work, he finally got his big break with the movie Dumb or Dumber. Of course, things only went uphill from there. He then was getting known by more and more people as one of the next big stars in Hollywood. Getting roles like "The Mask," "Liar Liar," "The Cable Guy," "The Truman Show," "The Grinch," and so many other ones in the following years. Like Tony Robbins, he started and lived in poverty for the start of his life. But just like Robbins, Jim Carrey became one of the most respected and liked actors in Hollywood.

There are countless examples and stories on how people have gone from the middle-class mindset or how they made it from the bottom to being some of the most successful people in the world. However, I want to make it clear that you don't need a "crazy success" story to be well respected. You might come from a good neighborhood that doesn't have any gangs, violence, etc. and you still could be respected. The only reason I bring this up is because for some reason a lot of people respect self-made billionaires or people who have "made it" by overcoming extreme conditions.

On the other side, if someone who comes from an upper class, fancy neighborhood that had no troubles growing up or at the start of their career, but makes the same accomplishments or even more than someone who struggled more than them, people tend to respect them less. Why? Well, because in their minds they think that if someone comes from "royalty" or a high-class neighborhood and ends up being very successful, they think that's its daddy's money, that they inherited their wealth from their parents, they had it easy, they got a better start, etc.When in reality they could've had it bad too. You don't know what they went through, or what they had to sacrifice in order to get successful. Yes, they most likely will have it easier than someone who came from the bottom up, but they have their struggles too. Just remember this: **nobody can inherit $150 billion from their parents. Hint, Jeff Bezos.**

Although this book is dedicated to helping teens and people of all ages be successful and consider being an entrepreneur as a career choice, I want to mention and make it crystal clear that the middle-classworker mindset is NOT a bad thing. In fact, if it weren't for them the world would be HUGELY different. Think about it, your house was made by a worker that had a boss. Your toothbrush, hair comb, school/work building, car, and even your phone are made by people that are employed, although many daily devices are being made by machinery and artificial intelligence (AI). If not for them, you would've had to make everything that's yours, by yourself! **If you see someone working as a janitor, waiter, constructor, or anyone else who doesn't work at a fancy job or is an entrepreneur, be thankful. If it weren't for them, the world would be a whole lot different.**

WHAT'S YOUR PLAN?

You know enough and are ready to finally start your business. What's your plan? Well, the first thing to know is if you already have a job, DO NOT quit your job. **If you suddenly leave work and you don't have any or little money saved up, you'll most likely end up broke and looking for a job again, and you probably won't have many options at that point.** But say you're a teenager that doesn't have a job or source of income, should you go and find a job right away? Well, not necessarily. Something that many parents of teen's need to find out are, you DO NOT need a job to provide for yourself or start your business. It's been known and available to make money in your school, job, and almost everywhere else you spend most of your day.

There are so many revenue streams you can make in your day-to-day life. Although I'm going to get more into revenue streams and investments you can make no matter what age you are in chapter 4, I'll give you some revenue streams right now that almost anyone can do. Sneaker trading: sneaker trading is one of the most common and effective ways to make money in huge quantities. It's self-explanatory. You buy/trade for a sneaker that has more value than what you paid for it. Then find another buyer that will either give you something that is worth more value or more money that you originally paid. The reason I say this is one of the easiest ways to make money in huge quantities is because one, almost anyone can do it no matter your age,and reason two is because it's so easy to start. As long as you have a mobile device or something to connect to the world, you're able to start.

Go to "Offer Up" or any online selling app or website and start. It's as easy as that and you could also find physical stores that you can find items to make a profit from. Such as Ross and any other retailer store that have shoes for cheap. I'll sometimes go to Ross (or any thrift store) and go to the shoe section just to look at what is so cheap and what I can sell. As always, there are so many things that are easy to flip for more than twice the profit. Of course, you need to know what you're doing and how to find out if something will sell or not, but again, all of this will go into more depth in chapter 4.

Anyway, back to the point of keeping your job. The reason to keep your job or in better words "have money" is because you need it for your basic needs. If you don't have any money to provide for your home, food, car, and transportation, you'll end up broke. And if things go worse you can end up like Chris Gardener (although you might not be able to get as successful or get back to where you were). Instead, have enough savings to last you at least one year. Bill Gates, the founder of Microsoft, and once the richest man alive said in a talk that when he was the CEO of Microsoft he always wanted to make sure the company had enough money to last them at lead a year. You might need more or less depending on your situation, but have close to a year in savings (food, shelter, phone, etc.).

That's the first thing to have for your business/life plan. What's next? Know where you're headed. **Knowing where you're headed or "clearly know your goal/vision" is one of the most important things you need to know to be successful. But that's the part where many people fail to learn, know, and find out.** The BSA or more commonly known as The Boy Scouts of America have a huge influence on boys around the nation (I suggest joining a pack if you're a young or if you're a full-grown teen, the venturing crew).

I remember clearly when I was a tenderfoot (one of the ranks) and my pack was on a camping trip. After we were done setting up camp we started to get into the "fun stuff". We cooked, explored, went to a nearby site-seeing place. After we were done, we came back to our campsite and started to settle down. My legs were done, and I was extremely tired. Around midnight my friends and I decided it would be cool if we went up to a cliff in front of our campsite. What could go wrong?

It was right in front of my tent and we had flashlights. Stupidly we went. We started to go up the hill more and more until we reached close to the top. Just as I was going to go back down, I saw this beautiful view of a nearby lake. I felt the wind breeze across my face and a blissful sound of silence. It was the best view I've ever seen. I wanted to stay for another couple of minutes, I told my friends to wait, but at that point they were bored and just left.

After a few minutes I decided to go back down to my camp. I went down and down and down, not knowing if I was going the right way. Five minutes later I found myself lost and without any equipment like a compass, map, or phone. Somehow my pack found me in the middle of the forest preserve in about ten minutes.

They took me in, and I knew for a fact that I was going to get yelled at. When my pack leader came up to me, he wasn't mad at all, in fact I might have thought he was furious because he wasn't saying anything. A few seconds went by till I asked him, "Mr. Karge, do you want me to go to my tent or…" He said, "No…Why did you leave in the middle of the night?" I didn't know what to say so I just paused. Then he said something that helped me so much in life. "No, I'm not mad that you left. You're a kid, you're supposed to have fun, but you should have known what you were going to do and where you're going to do it before you act upon it. Before you went to the woods, you should've brought either a compass or your phone."

That was a long story, I know, but take this from it. **If you're going to do anything in business, know where you're headed, where you're going to settle on, the market, your main customers, the numbers, etc.** If you want to start a blueberry pie business, then know exactly how and why you're going to do it. Even to the little things in life. If you cook your dinner and the pan is hot but you decide to pick it up, know where you're going to place it beforehand.

DO IT

Now you have enough money saved up and you know exactly what you're going to do, why you're going to do it, and you know the statistics in your new business, etc. Now what? DO IT. I can't stress enough how people tell me their idea for a new business, but they end up putting it in their back of their mind and forget about it. I know that the situation you're in makes it hard or difficult to start a new business, but there's a simple solution to that. Shelf it. **Shelfing something means to keep that idea in mind but never forget about it. Instead, when you're in the right time or position you want to be in, then unshelf it and start to make it into a reality.** Make sure you write it down somewhere you look at every day, like your phone or your refrigerator.

I mentioned that many people I know tell me their

new idea for a business, but they end up forgetting about it. Shelfing something doesn't mean to say, "Oh, well, I can't do it, plus it's a bad time." No, all it means is to keep that idea in mind and when you're ready to start, unshelf it. I want you to understand that shelfing something is the worst-case scenario--don't leave an idea waiting, instead make it a reality.

Again, remember shelfing an idea is WORST CASE SCENARIO. The bottom line is, don't procrastinate on your dream or just say that you'll start it. Actually DO IT.

You Got this!

In total, what are the three things to have and know before starting a business? One, have enough money saved up for close to a year for food, clothing, shelter, etc. Have something to keep yourself from ending up in a broke before starting. Try to shy away from the idea of plan B, because it makes your brain believe that no matter what happens, you'll be fine or, in other words, makes you soft.

Two, know where you're headed. Clearly define what your new business is, how you're going to operate it, your target base, all the financials, etc. Have a spreadsheet on what your business is and how you're going to make it successful. Know what you're getting into beforehand.

Lastly, DO IT. **Don't procrastinate to make your dream a reality. Start as soon as possible. It's alright not to pinpoint everything to the max. You don't need to, just come as close**

as possible and start. Of course, you're going to fail miserably but that's how it works.

Also try to forget about all the pampering your parents did to you when you were a little kid because, if you don't, you might end up giving up too easily because your mom said, "Don't worry little Timmy, you'll get there someday. How about we get some ice-cream?"

I want to give you something to always remember when starting a business: **Enjoy it, have fun with it, make it something you want to do. Business is something that if anyone wants to start one or join one, they need to have fun with it or at the very least not hate it. There's always going to be times where it could be hell or something goes wrong, but always remember to keep moving forward and start to make your dream business into a reality. If you don't, you end up living in the worker mindset.**

CHAPTER THREE

SCHOOL

"Some people are good in school, and some are good in life."

~Anonymous Author

———————

IS SCHOOL BAD OR GOOD?

School. We finally came to the point of discussing one of the most controversial things that people argue about. Is school bad or is it unfair? School is something I'd like you to discuss with an open mind, and be free to new ideas, no matter what opinion you have on it. However, I'm not going to sugar-coat it. I have certain beliefs about school and how the education system works. You might not agree with everything I say, and that's ok. In fact, I encourage you to have your own beliefs and not be changing opinions all the time. I just wanted to briefly state that although we most certainly have different views on things, we both also have to be open minded to new ideas.

To figure out what value (if any) school gives us, we first need to know what school is and what their goal is for students and children worldwide. By definition, school is *"an institution for educating children"* and *"any institution at which instruction is given in a particular discipline."* Ok, so the basic idea of a school is to teach various subjects to children while making sure they're disciplined. I'm pretty sure you also had the same idea. So far, so good, school's whole idea is to teach the basics of the most important subjects you need for life. Although most school subjects are pretty useless after grade 6.

Let's dig deeper on what the school systems goals are. In an article written by (gocorderz.com) they interviewed

12 teachers that taught grammar in elementary, junior high, high school, and college. The teachers' ultimate goal for all students was to learn and the goal for the school system to teach. *"To impart knowledge and skills and prepare people for the real world... that's the ultimate goal in my book,"* is what Miss Khan said when one of the interviewers asked her.

Another response was *"Innovation. Making things better for our world. We have to teach kids this innovative mindset. Set them up for success for THEIR future!"* Ariel Jankord continued, saying, *"Teachers should empower students to maximize their potential, discover passions, and help them as collaborate, critical thinkers."* The last quote I'm going to state is by Guy Tordjman. He said, *"For each student to receive the right tools, through education and in school, to fulfill his own dreams, goals, and desires."* What do you think about their goals? I don't know about you, but I say those are the perfect answers when anyone asks any teacher what is the ultimate goal for school.

They talked about preparing kids for the real world and the challenges along with it, to make the world a better place for them, and to create a basis for the kids dreams, hopes, and goals. All of them were amazing responses, and I'm guessing all those teachers genuinely want to do what they say, and that's great. But the question is, does the school system truly encourage this in their schools? I mean, think about it, do schools really incorporate these goals of making the dreams of the kids into their reality?

In my experience that never happens, especially if the school itself shys away from that idea. Almost all the teachers I've had never believed in me and my goal in life which was to be able to retire at 25, and to be one of the most respected CEO's in the world, along with many other things. And it wasn't like I was actively trying to tell people or teachers what my goals were. At one point in my early years of school, I was slightly arguing with a couple of kids in my classroom. Something about the subjects the school taught us with me complaining that I had career goals that didn't require school.

As we got more heated up in the conversation, our English teacher came over to our table and stopped us in our tracks. She started to trash down on me, saying that I was being disrespectful to her and my school. As usual, I got a detention and got sent to the principal's office while the other kids defending the school got no punishment whatsoever. Why? Because I disagreed with a teacher's job and the way the place she works teaches students to learn?

I'm not going to act like I was the victim, or that I was scarred for life, because I was setting myself up to get yelled at by a teacher. However, with full confidence I will say that what that teacher did wasn't positive to the goals I had. It's common with kids to get criticized by their teacher about their goals if they sound crazy and unachievable to the teachers. Ask a group of kids if they've had goals that teachers or school workers have shut down or were told that it was impossible to achieve. Most likely you'll get the majority of the kids that give countless examples of it.

Again, I don't want to claim that all teachers are against their kid's dreams, goals, and careers. It's never their fault; no teacher in the world comes with a mindset that everything a kid says is impossible to create, or to achieve. Instead, what happens is that they get taught by their own teachers, peers, and parents that their own dreams were impossible to achieve. So, in return, when they start to teach, they have a mindset that no dream is possible to achieve. That's one factor that goes into the reason that teachers teach like they've always done and have never adapted to change.

The second factor is the one that really does convince them that no crazy dream is possible. That second factor is that teachers haven't adapted to the new world and innovations that allow people and kids to become multi-millionaires, just by having fun. They never had any type of social media platform like YouTube, Facebook, TicTok, Twitter, and even Sound Cloud, along with many others. Those platforms have allowed kids to become famous around the world by just posting a video of them on one of those platforms. YouTube made an eight-year-old over $20,000,000 in less than a year with Ryan Guan's YouTube channel, Ryan's World, and his channel having over 25 million followers.

Another platform that has created opportunities for teens has been TicTok. TicTok has made a 15-year-old girl into multi-millionaire, in the case of Charlie D'Amelio, with Charlie appearing in a Super Bowl commercial with Jennifer Lopez! She now has over 60 million followers in her TicTok account, with just one sponsored post costing $100,000. I just listed some of the many examples of people who got started off of social media, but I'll list a couple more people who got started from social media and made it BIG.

Shawn Mendes made videos on Vine with his songs, which earned him a huge following at the time with 300,000 followers. He then got signed with a record studio with some huge studios like Sony Records, Warner Brothers, and Atlantic Records trying to get him. Charlie Puth got recognized by Ellen DeGeneres' record label in 2011 because of his cover of "Someone Like You" from Adele on YouTube. He's now signed with Atlantic Records and made huge hit songs like See You Again, One Call Away, We Don't Talk Anymore, Marvin Gaye, and countless others. Mr. Beast (Jimmy Donaldson) has a following of over 35 million and is one of the most respected YouTubers in the world. He's made crazy donations in the past with one of his videos donating $1,000,000 to one of his competitors in his challenges, and has raised $20 million for Team Trees. He's been sponsored by Honey, Quidd, War Robots, and many others.

There are countless people I could name that had their lives changed by social media but what's the point of all of this? Most school teachers (especially old ones) don't realize that kids can make millions of dollars and have their life changed at such a young age, without going to school or even graduating high school. They have a mindset that the only way kids can be successful is by getting a college degree and having the best grades possible. You can't blame them; as I mentioned before, teachers have been taught that there was only one way to be successful in their life which is going to college and graduating with a masters. The school system is trying to do good for students all over the country, but they have to adapt to the world we live in and the ways to make a successful living.

WHAT IS THE PROBLEM WITH SCHOOL?

What are the many problems school have, and why do they need to fix those problems? Schools all over the country and world get hated on by almost all students that attend them, but why? Well, school is the place to learn new things and be excited to learn them. School should be a place where both the teachers and students are happy to go, not somewhere kids dread going to. School needs to adapt and figure out new ways of teaching that will truly make the kids excited to learn the subject that is being taught.

Think about when you were in school, do you remember good experiences in that school? Maybe you do, maybe you don't. However, I'm almost certain that a lot of your schools' memories were lost or forgotten. Do you remember clearly the times where you were being taught a subject about math or any subject for that matter? It's crazy to think that although the whole basis of school is for you and the students to remember everything that they're being taught, they almost never remember the things that teachers told them to remember, besides the basics like multiplications and reading skills. It's even crazier that schools teach things that should help students with life, work, and with anything outside of school, but 90 percent of the truly important things being taught to students are never used!

You hear this time and time again (schools never teach subjects that are truly important to the students' lives and subjects that will help them outside of school) by siblings, TV, and any other successful person. So, what is the reason you should be learning this? None really. I'll be explaining further on the reason why schools don't adapt to change later on, but for now I want you to think of the reason like a slot machine. A slot machine has a bunch of different options that you can spin and land on, but if you want to get a certain option like a "cherry" you're going to have to spin it a couple of times. If you want to hit the jackpot, you're going to have to spin it a whole lot of times before you get even close to hitting it.

How does this correlate to schools? Think of the player and the guy pulling the lever as the schools in the system. All the options on what you can end up getting are the different subjects that schools teach. One could be math, the other could be English, and another could be history. The screen or the line that tells you what option you got are the kids. Each kid goes through every option on the slot machine, but ultimately ends up getting and picking three. That's just like the school system, because instead of spinning through the machines options, the kids are spinning through all the options (subjects) the schools teach them when ultimately they're only going to need three things that they learned from school that will be integrated in their career option.

An easier way to say it is they both go through a bunch of options when in reality; they're only going to land/need three things out of all the options they went through. Schools teach their students a bunch of subjects, tests, quizzes, and homework that will stress them out when in reality, they're only going to use and remember 1-3/100 things they learn about for their career. It's not getting any better, by the way. Now in the year of 2020 (and whatever year you're reading this in), there's becoming way more options and ways to make money and for a career that will pay a lot more money than a regular desk job.

As I talked about earlier, there are people becoming millionaires and getting known because of a platform like TicTok and YouTube that doesn't require people to show up at a certain time and doesn't require a boss. I've given you dozens of examples of people who have done this. It's not a dream anymore to work from home and make way more money at home than a regular job.

If you ask any kid what the top five jobs are that they want to explore, I'm betting that YouTuber will be pretty high up there. Especially if you ask a teenager and kids who are older. They almost will never say doctor, lawyer, accountant, or anything like that. Instead they come up with better jobs, those they can actually make money from now. Schools aren't teaching things that will actually help kids with the career they pick.

Instead, they teach kids useless information that won't be used in the kid's future. Everything from fifth grade up is almost useless to a kid's needs for their future career choice and in their real life. Everything besides adding, subtracting, multiplication, division, basic reading knowledge, and any of the basic knowledge to start off a kids life is non important and doesn't relate. Instead, they should reinforce the basics like reading, multiplication, etc., and make those things really good. Not just teaching kids things that won't help them in the short and long run.

They don't even have to teach the basics for half of the kid's time in the school system. Teach the kids the basics until fifth grade, and after that let them choose what they want to learn. The reason I say kids should choose what they want to learn beginning in fifth grade is because kids need to experience things and have more options to choose from at an early age. If schools change their way of teaching and let the kids decide what they want to learn, every single kid is going to change their opinion on what they want to learn, guaranteed. And that's a good thing, because now they'll now know what they do and don't like at an early age, so when the time comes to choose their career, they know exactly what they do and don't want to do.

However, kids have that choice of learning what they want at one point in their life. In high school, students have more freedom to choose what they want to learn but the problem with that is one, they're now getting pressured by their parents because after they graduate high school it's college. If they do end up going to college, it's going to be way more difficult to change their career choice because now they have to pay for their education, and they can't change their choice all the time.

The second reason why high school isn't the best time for kids to start to pick what they want to learn is because there aren't many options to pick from. Although it may seem like a lot of options, to kids it all revolves around the basic subjects of math, reading, and history. The only things besides the basic options is business education, art education, and sports education.

Now look at the other scenario, say schools did allow kids to start picking what they want to learn as early as fifth grade; it would be way easier for the kids to say what they want to learn, so when the time of high school comes, they don't need to worry about what they do and don't like because by that time they will already have had three or four years of experience with what they like or not, without worrying if it's too late. I know I spend a bit of time on this subject, but I can't stress enough how much better the school system could've been if they simply allowed kids to pick what they want as early as fifth grade.

Back to the problems schools have--they have various things that are of no use and things that make kids hate going to school. The biggest and most obvious problem school causes for kids of all ages, and especially high school and up, is stress. Stress is caused left and right by the work teachers give the students. Most recognizable of the things that cause students stress is a heavy workload, upcoming tests and quizzes, participation (things like embarrassment, trouble in the area, shyness, etc.), less time to relax or downtime, lack of communication, along with so many other things.

I wonder why so many kids have depression, anxiety, mood swings, and stress in general. I'm not by any means saying that schools should "go easy" on kids and not push them to their limit. That's what schools are meant for; they're meant for students to reach their limits and learn as much as they can while becoming smarter day after day. But the way they're pushing kids to their limits is so wrong, and there are better ways to do it. Kids should always be happy and excited to participate in every subject and excited to go to school in general. Not dread and hate it. Kids go into school with a mind that is ready to learn and get stuffed with.

The problem is that they always come out with a stuffed and filled mind that is always gassed out. The students are almost always tired after school and barely have the energy to do homework, assignments, and anything else in their own lives. That's some of the biggest issues and problems schools have. They cause stress, anxiety, hatefulness toward the school, overload of work, wrong teaching methods, wrong subjects, no freedom to allow kids to pick a subject that they want to learn, and much more. I can go on and on about the problems schools have and how they should change this and how they should change that, but at the end of the day the whole point of this is to let you become aware, and ways you can make it better.

So, what's the biggest thing you can do to make your days at school better? Make the most out of it. Yes, it's really basic and so simple, but it's the truth. I'll go deeper into it in the end of the chapter but for now just remember that school is something that you should make the most of. If you come into school thinking it's going to be a bad day then it will. If you go in saying you're going to make the best out of it, then

THE BIG IDEA - THE ROADMAP TO ENTREPRENEURSHIP

your school day will always become better. You need to make the most out of it always and find the best parts of it.

OTHERS HAVE BUILT SUCCESSFUL BUSINESSES

There have been a bunch of people I talked about in the earlier part of this chapter, but now I'm going to talk about the most successful people in the world that have gotten to the billions or created something amazing for mankind without a college degree.

Bill Gates, the founder/co-founder of one of the biggest companies in the world, Microsoft, is the third richest person in the world with a net worth of about $110 billion. Yeah, that's a tremendous amount of money, but what you might have not known is that he never graduated from college. To think that our school system teaches kids from kindergarten all the way up to high school, that you need a college degree to be successful in life.

Another self-made billionaire is Richard Branson, co-founder of The Virgin Company. He has a net worth of $4 billion, and guess what? He never went farther than high school, and on top of that, he is also dyslexic! He has made a name for himself and his company even though he never graduated high school. Now, what do you think is a better way to be remembered. Go through years of school and get remembered by your family members because you saved lives as a doctor or do you want to be remembered by the whole world by changing the way of transportation and aircraft travel. Branson has not only made a name for himself across the world, but he ended up becoming a billionaire in the process.

Jack Ma, the founder of Alibaba applied to Harvard University 10 times and not once did he get accepted. He went on to try finding a job in KFC--24 people applied and only 23 were accepted. He was the only one out of everyone who got rejected. At that point some may think to give up. How can someone take the embarrassment of getting rejected from KFC? Not Jack Ma, he then went on to start his own company, Alibaba, an e-commerce company that distributes manufacturing goods to business's around the world. After being rejected from Harvard and a fast food place, he created one of the biggest online commerce stores in the world. He retired from Alibaba in 2018 with a net worth of $42 billion!

This list could go on and on of people who have become very successful in their field, or have become billionaires, but I'm going to mention a couple more of them that have not graduated any further than high school or college. Michael Dell, highest form of education- one year of college, net- $23.5 billion. Henry Ford, highest form of education- 8th grade, net- $200 billion (in today's money). Ellen DeGeneres, highest form of education- one semester of college, net- $400 million. John D. Rockefeller, highest form of education- high school, net $340 billion (in today's money). Kim Kardashian, highest form of education- high school, net- $175 million. Jay-Z, highest form of education- high school, net- $1 billion. Leonardo DiCaprio, highest form of education- high school, net- $260 million. Emma Stone, highest form of education- high school, net- $30 million. Mark Whalberg, highest form of education- high school, net- $300 million. Drake, highest form of education- high school, net- $150 million.

These examples and stories show that you don't need a high IQ or degree to be successful in life. **You instead need a clear vision on what you want to accomplish, whatever it may be, know how you're going to achieve your goal, and start to make it a reality.** Yes, thinking that you're an entrepreneur and being one are very different. You can't just say you're going to accomplish your goal; you need to start it and work hard for it which is why many people give up on their dream. If you're in high school right now and don't know what you're going to do with your life and are scared about the world, don't worry. I'm not saying to not think about and look into your real-life realities, but don't overstress about it.

In the case that you just want to pass your grade until you know what you want to do then get C's. You definitely don't need to get straight A's to be successful in life, and especially in business. My parents agree with me that I should just get enough of a grade to pass. Nothing extraordinary, but just enough. School is something that could be a steppingstone for your success, or it could be something that can distract you from it. It just depends on the way you look at it and what you want to do. Again, if you want to be anything besides a lawyer, doctor, engineer, or any of the other degree-required jobs, school is going to distract you from your ultimate goal. On the other side of the coin, if you want to be the best engineer in the world or the best marketer or the best anything else in the world that requires an education, then your goal is to have the best grades.

It's proven that you can become successful without having any higher form of education than high school and, for some, no education at all. This sounds cringy but if they can do it, you can do it. What's stopping you from dropping out? Mom, dad, sister, brother, guardian, family, friends, teacher, or anyone/anything else that want you to get the highest form of education possible and wants you to go to college—their opinions don't matter at all. Why should you care what they think? If they want you so badly to graduate college with straight A's then they should do it themselves. Why are they worrying so much about your education if they're not going to get impacted by it at all? That's the thing with a lot of people in this world.

You can become one of four people in this world. A critic (A critic is a legless man who teaches how to run. Channing Pollock), a talker (talk gets you nowhere, action gets you anywhere. Anonymous), a dreamer (a dreamer is someone who only finds his way by moonlight, and his punishment is that he sees the dawn before the rest of the world. Oscar Wilde) and a doer (The world had plenty of dreamers but it's the doers that shape the planet. Tim Fargo). The question is, which one are you?

WHAT SHOULD THEY/YOU DO?

What should school do instead, what are the things school should adapt to, what should you do? In this part of the chapter I'm going to list what school is useful for, and if you should pursue school. We first need to look at what school is truly useful for, whether you have to graduate college or not. Basically, what is useful for everyone when it comes to school? By far, one of the most important things school provides for you is the ability to socialize almost every day. I know some friends/people that are homeschooled and, unfortunately, are not very social. Socializing in school allows you to talk to one another without worrying if the person you're talking to will affect your life. If you get bullied or get criticized by someone in school, it's good because it'll show you a bit of how people are really going to talk and feel around you.

Obviously, you and I know that once you get out of school and head into the "real world," people aren't going to care or be concerned about you unless it affects them. If you cause something remotely bad to happen to them, they're not going to tell on you. They're going to cuss you out, hurt you, and may even do something back to you. Although it's sad, it's the truth, and because it's the truth, school will help you overcome that fear of getting ignored by others. In school if you tell on someone, they're going to call you a snitch.

Another thing socializing helps you with is that it allows you to find out how to talk to people in order to get something in return. Or, in other words, sales skills and being a good speaker. Being able to present yourself professionally is something everyone needs, no matter what their job is. Do you want someone to buy something from you? Use your sales skills. Is someone bashing you in front of your friends? Present and defend yourself. Looking for a job? Sell yourself (your image and skills) to the person interviewing you. Having sales skills and being able to present yourself in a professional matter is one of the most important things you can learn because it opens new opportunities and doors for you. And, by the way, school doesn't even teach you that directly, it just happens by talking to your peers and by accident.

Let's move on--what else school helps you with. This is something that probably is the most important thing school does, and helps students with; however, they approach it in the worst way possible. Making your brain think, learning. This is the most obvious answer anyone would say if you asked them what school helps you with. However, it's a bit more complex than you might think. The most important thing school does is making you think which in return makes your brain "grow" and become smarter by teaching subjects like math, English, history etc. Let me explain better.

Growing your brain and making it smarter helps you solve problems and overcome difficult situations. Schools do this by giving tests, reading books on a certain subject, quizzes, homework, learning about the subjects they teach, etc. It's such an obvious thing but schools approach it in such a bad way. By that I mean, although they make students think and use their brain to the full potential, but on the wrong subjects and platforms.

Instead of helping a kid solve a problem like, "What are some ways I can make myself stand out of a crowd when looking for a job," they want kids to find the square root of 169. Instead of showing kids sales skills and how to present themselves to others, they ask them what is the y-intercept of $4x+2y=12$? They make kids think and grow their brain on a platform that is useless everywhere besides the school.

Instead, they should teach or make students think on things that will actually help them in their life, like what are liabilities and assets, how to grow and even start their own business (if they would like), what are revenue streams, negotiating, public speaking, how to solve problems in the best way possible (outside thinking), handling money and accounting, manners, insurance policies, taxes, learning from past mistakes, and I could list countless more things that school should teach instead of what they currently teach.

Ok, so far we've got two things that schools help us with, (although they both either don't do it directly or do it in the worst way possible) socializing, and making us think and expand our brain. Well, what else is there? Personally, I can't really think about anything else school helps us with that will realistically help in our own lives, besides getting us to leave our house. I understand that school is extremely important to everyone and anyone, but if they could change their way of teaching it, it could be way more beneficial to children around the world. I personally think school should be a little more like this. They should teach kids what they are already teaching them up to fifth grade, and once they reach sixth, they should figure out what the students like and what they might want to do.

For example, if Sally likes to paint and has a huge passion for it then they should focus more on her drawing skills than learning how to cross-multiply fractions. Think about yourself. What do you want to ultimately achieve in your life, no matter what type of life you'll end up having, whatever that thing might be, schools should help you focus and learn more on how to achieve that goal. Another example is that if Alex likes business and wants to learn more about it and how to run one, then the school should instead focus more on how to help Alex learn more about entrepreneurship and business.

Same goes for little Jimmy; if he loves to code and program on the computer then help him learn about programming. The school system needs to adapt to change and help students achieve their own goal no matter what it is. That's something that can easily be fixed by the government, but they never want to fix it. I'll explain further in a second, but for now just know that this is a problem that can easily be fixed.

Again, I'm just a kid that knows and loves to talk and do business, so personally, I don't have a say on the school system's way of teaching, but now that we're in 2020, there's so many ways to learn about what you want to do. YouTube, Google, books and so much more. Whether it be learning how to craft a board or learning how to run a business, you can find it practically anywhere; but then again, that's just me.

WHY ISN'T IT DIFFERENT?

Something you need to know is that the school system purposely does this (not help their student achieve their dreams and teach different subjects that matter while adapting to the world they're in). The reason being is they want kids, teens, toddlers, and babies to grow up into the rat race. I talked all about the rat race and what it is in Chapter 2, but for a quick refresh, the rat race is a continuous cycle that people go through in their life.

They go to school and learn, go to college and try to graduate with the highest grades possible, get a job, car, spouse, family, and try to grow that job until they get to one of the highest positions possible. In the process, overtime they get a raise, their spending habits increase, and once they get an even higher raise, their spending habits also increase again, and it keeps going again and again and again. The rat race is what kids are getting taught by their family, teacher, and friends without them knowing it's the worst thing to do and they have other choices to pick from.

You might ask yourself, "Why don't they change the system if it's so corrupt?" Well, the reason is because the government doesn't want people to overachieve and because they need cooperations to succeed. Why do they want cooperation's to succeed? Because they need employees to work for them in various jobs such as labor (assembly lines), engineers, lawyers (suing the companies), carpenters, bankers, electricians, marketers, etc. and in return they all pay taxes. For example, if a corporation wants to open a new manufacturing company in another state, they need employees to do this and to do that, and who owns the land? The government! On top of that, they also want to look good to the press and public, if they have a new job opening, who's going to get all the credit? The mayor and the government. People are needed always, even when we find new ways to make thing easier and faster, we still need people to do things computers can't.

This has been going on for hundreds of years. When the Egyptians were building the pyramids, who made them? People made them! They needed people to do the labor, they needed people to make the blueprints, they needed messengers, and they needed this and that. But, ultimately, what were those people called? Slaves. Nowadays people use other terms and ways to refer to employees by calling them workers, but the truth and reality is employees are modern day slaves.

Think about it, they (referring to employees and slaves) both have to answer to a boss or someone who's in charge, they both get little to no breaks, they both get the materials or tools to help the boss' company/country grow, they both have people working alongside them, they both get scheduled times to come in and out of work, and the biggest thing is that in return they get shelter and food/reward. How do companies do these nowadays you may ask yourself? Well, its easy and obvious. What do companies give you for your hard work? A check. And what do you get in return for that check? You pay for your house, food, insurance, transportation, taxes, etc. Just like slaves, that's what they did.

Obviously, things aren't as severe as they once were. Now we have our so-called "freedom" (because in reality they still have orders and if they don't follow them they'll get fired) because they can arrange our time schedule a bit more, they have days to themselves (like holidays), they can ask for more of a reward, like a check. The work isn't as severe, and a whole bunch of other things that allow more freedom to people.

If you're still not convinced that the rat race is real or that working for someone else is the only way possible, I want you to think about something. Say people did find out that they were modern slaves and that they were/are being treated worse than what they should be, what do you think would happen? There would be riots and protests going around everywhere in the country, and possibly the world. Do you honestly believe that the government wants people to riot, protest, and figure out that they're being taken advantage of?

It's crazy to think that--they want everyone to be in an endless loop that the government calls "The American Dream" which, in reality, is the rat race. It would be too much to handle. There's roughly 300 million people living in America and let's just say that only half of all people started protesting. That's 150 million people rioting the streets and with the US army only having 500,000 active duty personnel that's going to be hard to contain. Does the government want that to happen, NO.

So, if you still think that the government wants to help students create their dreams and goals into a reality and that school is just a begining stage to become part of the rat race, this book isn't for you. In total, things aren't better because the government and school system doesn't want it to change. They want people to go to school for over 20 years of their life and in all of those 20 years, they want kids to become part of the rat race.

WHEN DID IT ALL START?

When did the whole idea of the "American Dream" become a reality, when did people start to believe that having a degree was the way to become successful, and when was it useful, when wasn't it? The whole idea of having a degree to be successful wasn't always something that was popular and something where people thought that a degree, straight A's, and going to a college was the key to success. Everyone before that was farming, used crops, and never went to school. It all started as early as the 1800's! The time period where the whole idea of going to school and getting a degree to be successful or, in other words, entering the rat race, started in the industrial age.

The industrial age was where everything started, and it was when schools focused on raising kids into the worker mindset. The industrial age was when the whole world started to change for the better. Furthermore, it was when the US started to use new manufacturing processes between them and Europe at a huge scale. It was when businesses, corporations, factories, and where the Rockefellers of that time started to form and rise. The economy started to rise, and inventions started to form, like the factory machines, steam engines, telegraphs, typewriters, dynamite, the photograph, electricity generators, and so many other inventions that allowed factories and business to blossom and become giants in the world. How does the school system correlate to this you may ask? Well it all comes down to supply and demand.

Although everything started to blossom like the modern day factories, they needed not only the tools, but people. Factory owners needed workers to run the machines and make sure everything was going to plan. So, what do they do? They ended up changing the school system (not literally) to their advantage and made kids and their parents believe that getting a college degree was the key to success. As a result, people started to get the idea of the rat race jammed into their brain to the point where anything else, like starting your own business, was guaranteed disaster. Which in reality it was, back then things were different. Having monopolies was legal, and anyone could create one and keep it without worrying that it would be split apart.

If you were lucky enough to create a business and grow it to make it successful, you would get approached by the giants of your business (for example if you had a railroad company you would get approached by the Carnegie Steel Company). You than would be given two options. Option number one, you would sell your company to your higher competitor for a fairly good amount. Option number two, if you were to say no and decline selling your business, they would target and destroy your business.

This is one of the cleverest and fastest ways to kill your competition. This method still works today and if you were to do this yourself, I'm guaranteeing that you would kill your competition in a snap of a finger. If you were the company offering to buy a competitor's smaller company, this is how you would do it. You would compare your competitor's prices to your own. If you had higher or the same prices, you would drop your products' price so low until the point where you're losing money every time someone buys that product from you. This sounds bad so far, but as a result what's going to happen to your competitor? Nobody's going to buy from them!

For example, if you and your competitor had the same product listed for $0.20 for every 1,000 orders you've had, and each of you and your competitors' product cost $0.12 to make, then what you would do is drop your product to $0.10 for each 500 orders. Obviously you're losing money, but as a result, your competition would lose money as well. If you were in the position that you could buy the same product from three different companies; company number 1 is selling their product for $0.25 each for 1,000 orders. The second company is selling the same product for $0.18 each for every 1,000 orders. The last option is the third company; they sell the exact same product as the other two companies but instead they'll sell you their product for $0.10 each for every 1,500 orders.

What would you pick? Same products, same value, and same size the only difference is that they all have different options. If your answer is anything but company 3 something's wrong with you. You're obviously going to pick company 3. They have way better prices than the other two companies' and on top of that they'll give you more for less.

That's what the giants would do to their competition. Yes, they were going to lose a lot of money in the process, but it was only going to be temporary. By the way, this method of killing your competition only works if you're the giant of your field, and if you have a huge abundance of money beforehand. If you don't have both of those things, you'll be the one out of business. Back to the point of all this, if you were to start a business back than it would be almost guaranteed disaster. So, what sounded like a better option? Going to school for a quarter of your life, getting straight A's, and getting the highest degree possible sounded far more promising.

It wasn't guaranteed that you would automatically get a high paying job right away, but it was way better than starting your own business and having only a slight chance that you would either get bought out or that you would grow your company to be successful. Getting that "special" degree was the key to success and it was for years after.

I can't blame the people who worked for a company for years or the employees. This is also when people fell into the worker mindset. They started because of their family members. One person, the dad or the mom, would go to school from first grade to college. They would get a job at a factory as a worker and got paid little money compared to now, but the difference was that most people that went to school for the first time always worked for their parents and grew crops. They would never get paid much for the crops they grew. On top of that they never socialized with anyone besides people along with them in the farm (aka their family) so when they started working in the factories, they were able to socialize with people they have never met before. One of the biggest factors that played in also was that when they worked on the farm, they were always outside in the heat for most of the day. In the factories they were at least in a room that wasn't burning the employees with the sun.

For the workers, this was the best thing that ever happened to them. They got paid a lot more by the company than what they were used to in the farms, they got to socialize with people that they never met everyday due to work, and on top of all of that they weren't in the sun all day. All the benefits they had were worth it just for 20 years of their life. However, what happened after they got comfortable in their job--the "big boss" made an announcement to all the employees and said, "If you go to school again for a couple more years and work hard enough to get a better degree, in return I'll give you higher pay and you'll become more important to the company, but only if you get a better degree."

If you were in their position and were offered higher pay just for four years of schooling what would you do? I'm not going to lie, if I was in that time, that offer would sound promising considering the fact that I already have a good job compared to farming. What does the worker do? He goes to school again for the second time. After four years of hard work and studying he finally gets a better degree and goes back to the same boss he had previously. He gives the boss the better degree that was better than he's previous one. The boss says yes and he ends up giving the better job and paying the worker more.

The worker's all happy and gets excited for his new job that pays better and gives him better working conditions. A couple more years go by and the boss makes another announcement and says, "If you go to school again for four more years of your life and get another degree that's even better than the one you have now, in return I'll give you an even better raise and better working conditions. But only if you go to school and get another degree. If you don't, you won't get a raise." What does the worker think to himself? Oh my god! If I go to school another couple of years, I'll get an even better raise and better working conditions.

The man goes to the same school for another four years for the third time and starts to get a better education, trying to get that piece of paper that will earn the worker a better raise. After he graduates and gets his degree, he goes back again to the same job and presents the paper to the same boss who told him to get a better degree. The boss thinks about it and agrees to give the worker a better pay in return for getting the degree. YES, the man says, happy that he gets better pay and better working conditions. Although he's happier, he's starting to get older.

A couple of more years go by and by then the man has a good house, wife, kids, car, etc. He goes to work again one day and the boss gives another announcement to the workers, "If you get a better degree than the one you already have and go to school for another couple of years, I'll give you a better raise, and on top of that, after you retire I'll give you money, even if you're not working at the company anymore." The man is getting older now, pushing his 40s, and says to himself, "I could make even more money than I've ever had before if I just go to school one more time and I'll get paid when I stop working here." What does he do? He goes to school again for the fifth time in his life, just to get that degree.

Another four years go by to get the ultimate degree he needs for his best paying job ever. After he finally finishes his years at the school, he gets the degree and gives it to the boss and, finally, after so many years, he gets the highest paying job he could get. Here's the thing though, like any parent, they want their kids to become even better than they were and have fewer mistakes. The man tells his 15-year-old kid that if they go to school and get the degrees, they will have the best life ever, but instead he tells them to learn from his mistakes. He tells the kids to get the highest degrees ever and not wait for the boss to tell them to get a higher one. So, instead of waiting, the kids get the highest degree they can get as early as possible by the age of 30.

What do they do when they have their kids? They tell their kids to get their degree even earlier than he did. The same thing happens again and again and again until a decade later the parents are still doing the same thing of getting trapped into the rat race. This happens why, because of their parents and family members getting into the rat race at an early age without even recognizing they're in it.

This didn't change at all for a good couple of years; monopolies kept growing while more and more people started to become part of what we know today as the rat race. However, after the industrial era when Theodore Roosevelt was elected, things started to change. When Roosevelt became president, he started to stop monopolies from getting out of control. He created the Sherman Antitrust Act which basically meant that all monopolies that were controlling all their competitors and didn't leave a chance for others to start their own companies would be broken up into smaller companies or would be shut down.

This allowed other people to create their own companies without worrying of getting completely shut down by their other bigger and better competitor right away. Now people could start their own company and have a chance to make it become successful. You didn't need a college degree to start a business, so there wasn't really any need to go to college unless you wanted to become the basic people, like a doctor.

However, the thing that made people not start their own business was that they didn't realize that they could start one without being shut down. They were too scared and afraid of what happened before, when there were monopolies left and right so, as a result, they never wanted to, and didn't want to, take the chance of failure as with many other things. You would at least expect people to somewhat change and start to realize that, but they never did. The school system didn't change once, and to this day it hasn't. They still, to this day, haven't changed their mindset on teaching kids that there are other options to be successful, and they haven't changed what they teach besides minor changes.

WHAT IF YOU WANT TO START YOUR BUSINESS?

Say you're in high school and you want to drop out to start your dream business or just to work somewhere that you want to. It's completely up to you (if you're over 18), but if you just got motivated to start a new business you don't know anything about, first learn the specifics about it. You might not even like it, and only do it because you want to show off to everyone that you started your own business and brag about it. Then that's the right time to put a cap on it. Entrepreneurship is an awesome thing to have, but it's not a game. You need to be focused and dedicated on what you do, no matter what it is.

You could probably tell that I'm on both sides on leaving school or not, but one thing that I've learned, which is needed in life and in business, is that **you NEED to see and understand both sides of the coin. In whatever you do, see both sides of the coin. Even if you're making a decision on someone or something, you need to see both sides. If you**

don't, you could miss out on what could have been a better decision.

On one side you can drop out and have a good understanding on business and how to run one. You might have a great chance to succeed, but on the other side there is a high risk of not making it to the top and the reality of losing it all. Please apply this to yourself and in your life. If you don't, it won't be impossible to succeed in life, but it will be another obstacle in the way.

I want you to do an experiment that will show you if your school looks into business and if they want to teach it or not. If you're in middle school, and if your school has a library, the next time you go there, go look for a business, entrepreneurship, investing, stock, or real estate book. Nothing special, just a business or life book that will show you the basics of entrepreneurship. I'm guessing there's a pretty high chance you won't find one, especially if you're in a public school. One thing I've learned through my years in school, business, my books, and in audio books, is that school isn't meant to teach you about money.

Right now, as I'm writing this, I'm in school! Yeah, out of all places. A couple of hours ago I just got done taking my IRA testing (pretty much a test that shows what classes you'll be in next year) and guess what? No questions about how to do your taxes, how to make money, nothing about business or entrepreneurship. Of course, I might be exaggerating a bit because I'm currently in eighth grade, but nevertheless my point is crystal clear, school is NOT designed to teach you about money.

School instead was made to be a brainwasher for kids since the age of six! **They teach you how to write properly, how to do fractions, what ratios are, how to analyze Shakespeare, but not how to make your own business or how to make some money at an early age.** Think of it yourself. When was the last time your school taught you word-by-word how to start your business or anything that can help you with your dreams and goals. I personally can't remember, and so can't millions of people around the globe. School isn't meant for people who want to become interested in business, entrepreneurship, and almost anything besides any of the typical degree-needing jobs like doctor, lawyer, electrician, programmer, and etc.

I know for a fact that many people are disagreeing with what I say, and that's all right. Again, I always want to see both sides of the coin. It's not that school never allows you to learn about business, entrepreneurship, or anything else that you might find interesting. School does allow you to pick something that you like to do, for example, business advice and how to write in word and excel spreadsheets. Once you're in high school, there's a whole lot more options for you that will allow you to learn new things that you want to learn about.

That's great that once you enter high school you get to pick your own classes and so much better than what grammar, middle, and elementary school offers you. However, for one, that's not until high school and, two, it's the very tip of the iceberg on what really helps you with it and the truths of it. School is something that everyone has mixed thoughts about. You, your cousin, your parents, my parents, and everyone in the world have views and thoughts about school. If you disagree with someone or if they disagree with you about school or how it's taught, don't worry. Just leave them or make a fool out of them.

I already talked about the three things you need to start your own business earlier in this chapter, but this is something you always need to remember, no matter what you do. If you're starting your business, if you're in an argument, if you're deciding to blame someone or not, or anything else, what's important to remember is that you need to see both sides of the coin. Just remember this whenever you have a hard decision to make on someone, or an action you or somebody else did.

MAKE THE MOST OUT OF IT

At the end of the day, it's not really your decision if you want to go to school or not, it's your parents or guardians, so what should you do now that you know there's nothing in school that can really show you how to be successful in life without being in the rat race? Make the best out of it. Yes, this whole chapter I've been mostly disagreeing with what school is, and if it's really useful, but just like any situation, you have to make the best and most out of it. If you're in school and they're not teaching you anything that you need to know about what you want to achieve, or about the real world, make the most out of it.

How? Go to YouTube in-between classes and search business courses for free. Listen to them, learn from them, and take advantage of them. If you're in math class and have nothing to do, make that time the best by thinking of new business ideas and ways to make another revenue stream. If you're passing periods after you're done with class, go read a page of a business book or a book of anything that will help you achieve your goal. Hell, if you're in school and don't want to listen to something you already know, go and listen to an audio book.

Just remember that it's not certain you'll be caught by the rat race or you'll work at a job for your whole life if you graduate and get a degree. You can always get yourself into business and entrepreneurship, I don't care what age you are. Young, old, or a teenager, you can always learn new things both in life and in business. So, make the most out of it. Personally, I'm going to move both into a new house and school for freshman year. But let me tell you something, I'm going to enjoy the hell out of it no matter what happens.

Before I go any further, I'd just like to say thank you to all the teachers in the world. Although I hate the way the school system is, and I know there's different ways to make it better than it is, it's not the teachers' fault. They get told what to teach by the school they work for, and some of them want to change the way they teach. But then again, they don't have the choice of that which is really sad. Teachers, regardless what they teach, are needed all around the world and even I take them for granted.

There are kids in second and third world countries that don't even have the opportunity to learn how to read, write, do multiplications or add and subtract. We all should be grateful and not take things for granted. If you're in school and you want to drop out when legally allowed, then go for it. Just be sure to know what you're getting into, because I know a lot of people, even kids, that don't know the reality of business and the hardships of it. Learn as much information on what you're going to be doing from now on and try to master it or come as close as can be.

Remember that school isn't everything, and if you want to master a skill or business or job, it's not a necessity to have a piece of paper that says you're qualified. After reading this you know that there's countless ways to make money without a degree or recommendation by anybody. Justin Bieber did it, Charlie D'Amilio did it, Bill Gates did it, and countless others did it, so who or what should stop YOU from doing it. You might even want to start a business but just want to learn how to make more revenue streams and the truth about the rat race. That's fine; I encourage you to stick with what makes you happy (as long as it provides for your life). There's always time to learn new things no matter what it is. The only advantage the teenagers have while reading this, and older people don't, is time.

So, to top it all off, if you're in school, work, or in anything you're doing always remember to take advantage of it and to make the most out of it. At the end of the day you have to remember that school is something you should be thankful for, because if you even have the chance to go to any school whether they teach business, entrepreneurship, or something you want to achieve and accomplish, you're already in one of the best starts in both the world and in life.

CHAPTER FOUR

INVESTMENTS & REVENUE STREAMS

"Never rely on one flow of income."

~Grant Cardone

———————

WHAT ARE REVENUE STREAMS?

If you're new to business or in the financial world in general, you might be asking yourself what are revenue streams, and why is a whole chapter dedicated to it? Well, revenue streams are one of the most important things you need in order to live and pay for things you need. Revenue streams are "a source of revenue from a company, organization, or person."

In other words, revenue streams are the different ways a person or company gets the money to pay for their needs. For example, for most people all over the world, their revenue stream is their job, no matter what type of job it is. For others it's their company or business that acts like a revenue stream to them. Revenue streams are any type of way to get money coming into the person or company, so there can be dozens of revenue streams they can have. Let's use Samsung as an example. Samsung sells dozens of products like electronics, televisions, laptops, mobile phones, refrigerators, printers, etc. All the products they sell are revenue streams for them and the more revenue streams they have is more money coming in to them.

However, I'd like to mention, before we get any further, that in some cases having too many revenue streams can be bad for a company. I'll get into more detail later on, but a quick reason why having too many revenue streams is bad is because in case a company has to many products (aka revenue streams) they sell, their customers or interested buyers won't know what they're known for, or what their main product is. This makes a company appear to people that they are not secure on what they sell and what they're whole company is based around. In some cases, this works for the company instead of working against them, but this only happens to stores like Target, Wal-Mart, Pete's Market, and any other type of retail or grocery store.

The importance of revenue streams is huge because in the case that a company or person doesn't have enough revenue streams, it could break them and force them to turn to debt or not making them profitable. How many revenue streams do you have? You might have a job if you're of age and maybe a side hustle that are your only revenue streams. I'm also going to get more into the statistics of people that have revenue streams later on, but for now I'll ask you this. How many revenue streams do you think the average American has? I also want you to ask yourself how many revenue streams the average millionaire and billionaire has. I'll tell you the answer later on in this chapter but ask yourself that question.

Anyway, I'll give you some examples of why having multiple streams is hugely important. One example, and the most obvious one, is when a person gets fired. When someone gets fired from their job, they won't have any money coming in for the things they need and for most people the only way they get money is their job. So, what are they going to do if they get fired? Although they can always get another job, it's hard for them to get the same position and pay their old job gave them, especially if they were in higher position than others at their old job. If you or your parents get fired all of a sudden by their boss or whomever they work for, you and or your parents won't have any money coming in.

Everything follows, such as being unable to pay for groceries, not being able to afford the car, then phone bills come in, and on top of everything else, the mortgage won't be paid for. You'll be broke! The next example is a financial crisis. In the case that the state, city, or country you're living in a financial crisis. That's exactly what's happening right now as I'm writing this. As I mentioned in an earlier chapter about a pandemic going around the world, it's still going on and has gotten worse because the second wave of the virus is hitting hard.

Back to the point that, yes, things always get better, just like the crises of 2008 with more than 10 million people losing their homes, the great depression of the early 1930's, the 1973 oil crises with almost no gas and common shortages of it happening day after day, and the pandemic of 2020 having 36.5 million Americans lose their jobs in less than two months.

Eventually everything got better sooner or later. However, in the time of the crisis whether you like it or not, things are going to get worse for a lot of people, especially for single parents or parents that only one of them works for the family. So, what are they going to do in the high chance that they get fired? This is where having different multiple streams come in.

HOW MANY REVENUE STREAMS SHOULD YOU HAVE?

Having multiple revenue streams is as easy as this. Say there's two people, Mike and Scott. Scott has an amazing job with an average salary of $200k a year with a 401k and a savings account. He works as a manager at an investment firm. On the other side, Mike doesn't have a "regular" job like Scott does. Although he doesn't have one main job, instead he has a bunch of little businesses that provide for him. One is a cleaning service, another is a navigation app, he has a business that cleans trucks, and another is a chain of ice cream machine trucks. He also has another app that is a game for both children and adults, and the last income stream is selling websites.

In all, everything Mike does brings an annual income of $100k. Scott lives in a bigger than average house, worked at his job over 40 years (he is 60 years old), and often vacations with his family. Mike on the other side rarely has any vacations, doesn't have a wife or family, never has any business more than five years, he's 40 years old, and lives in a small house. Suddenly the world goes through financial crises because of a virus and all the stock both Mike and

Scott have loses almost all its value! Both small and large businesses are going bankrupt and people are starting to get laid off.

Two months go by and people are still getting laid off, businesses are going bankrupt, and there is almost no improvement in the chance of securing Scott's job. Ultimately, Scott loses his job and almost all of Mike's businesses go out of business. They both lose a big source of money coming in for both of them. Like any person, Scott looks for a job that pays enough to provide for his family. Day after day he goes to interviews, looks for job openings, and everything in the middle. Still, after so many months of looking for jobs, Scott can't find a job that pays enough for his family and it's even harder when the whole world goes into quarantine to avoid getting the virus.

Mike's also is suffering with many of his customers and business that he had before the crises are starting to leave, and some already left him. Everything stays the same for the next couple of weeks, but eventually something starts to change. Kids, teenagers, and adults all over the world start to get bored with their house being closed and not being able to go to any public events or visit their friends house due to quarantine. As a result, they start to download apps and games into their phone to play.

As I mentioned before, Mike created an app that was a game dedicated for kids, teens, and adults. More and more people start to download and play Mike's game. Over time, the game becomes a trend for people to play and almost 5 million people play and use the app consistently! Mike now has way more than enough money for his bills and anything he needs to pay for. Back to Scott, he finally gets a job as a manger! However, Scott got a job as a manger in a retail store making nothing close to what he used to make.

At the end of the year, Mike's app turned out to be one of the bestselling game apps ever. And on top of that, his other businesses start to get in higher demand for their service. Both his ice cream trucks and his website businesses start to attract more and more customers. Now, Mike has different revenue streams coming in left and right, while Scott is still working as a retail store manager. Yes, I know, this story was a long one but what was the lesson of it? Although it's obvious, the lesson to be learned in this story is that **it's hugely important to have multiple and different revenue streams no matter what job you have. Having multiple revenue streams are important because in the case that something happens, that causes you to lose your business, job, or whatever you're working for, you'll always have something else to provide for you.** In Mike's case his app was what worked for him.

Imagine if he'd never had that app to make money for him. His app was just one revenue stream that Mike had. Say his app did end up failing and nobody wanted to play it or even downloaded. He still had six other businesses to support him. His ice cream shop could've been worth a lot

THE BIG IDEA · THE ROADMAP TO ENTREPRENEURSHIP

more if kids went out more (once the pandemic ended). The website business Mike had has a higher chance to succeed once more as more people stay at home and try to start their own businesses. In the other case, say all three of Mike's business failed, HE STILL HAS THREE MORE! Those three more companies that Mike has are still way more revenue streams to lean back on. He could always sell them, focus on one of them, partner with another company for them, and so much more!

I'm going to get more into detail about the statistics later on but a quick thing to know is that the average millionaire has at least 7 revenue streams from their different businesses. Compare that to the average American or to the average person in the world, which had almost nothing! Only 1-2 revenue streams the average person from America has, ONLY 1-2 (based on their job and any other side hussle)! Think about it, how many revenue streams do you have?

Back to the point, those are only two examples of why you need multiple revenue streams and I can go on and on about so many different reasons why you need a lot of revenue streams but here are a few more. Injury (in the case that you break a bone, for example), family emergency, the company your working for (or the main way you get you revenue from) fails or goes bankrupt leading to not being able to pay you, higher expenses in your day-to-day life, if you make a bad decision in your job/business, and so much more! If only one of those cases were to happen to you, you're destined to need another job, business, and revenue stream coming in to pay for the things you need.

Think about this yourself and if one of the things I listed happened to you. Would you be able to pay for things you need or, better yet for teens, would you be able to afford the things you want. Of course, there's way harsher and worse things that could happen, however these are just a few. That's why you need multiple revenue streams in your life, business, and anything else you do. Please, make sure to create more revenue streams and in the case that you already have multiple revenue streams, make sure that you give it your all. **More revenue streams = less chances of crisis for you** - Alex Jimenez.

MULTIPLE REVENUE STREAMS

Let's take a trip to Miami, Florida, where one of the giants in sales, real estate, business development, and social media lives--Grant Cardone. He's known around the world as the best real estate expert and has raised over a BILLION DOLLARS in assets for his clients over at Cardone Capital. On top of that, he's written eight books that have sold globally while including his 10X method in them.

One of his biggest accomplishments is creating the annual 10X growth conference (a HUGE conference in Vegas about the strategies of the best entrepreneur, actors, and singers). His recent speakers being Kevin Hart, Magic

Johnson, Elena Cardone, Snoop Dog, Steve Harvey, John Maxwell, Daymond John, Tia Lopez, and many more. He's also the CEO of Cardone Training Technologies (helps businesses grow in sales, social media, etc.) while being the CEO/partner in six privately held companies helping millions of people whether it's in his books, programs, or conferences along the way.

Yes, he was very successful in the past and notice that while I was giving you the rundown of him, I mentioned a TON of revenue streams that he has. As I mentioned before, the average American only has around one or two revenue streams, such as their job and their 401k (which you can't redeem until retirement).In contrast, the average millionaire has seven revenue streams--stocks, real estate, patents, dividends, businesses, advertisements, royalties, etc.

DIFFERENT REVENUE STREAMS

I'm going to break this down into three parts. 1 is the beginner, and applies to almost everyone that has permission by their parents. It's easy to do while not requiring too much work. 2 is the intermediate--the intermediate doesn't need much to start although they need internet and some startup money. 3 is the advanced. The advanced is for the people who have time on their hands while having internet/startup money.

```
        BEGINNER                        INTERMEDIATE

 Voiceovers    Logo      Ghost Rider   Youtuber   Influencer   Podcaster
               Designer
```

```
                    ADVANCED

            Stock      E-Commerce    Web
            Trader                   Designer
```

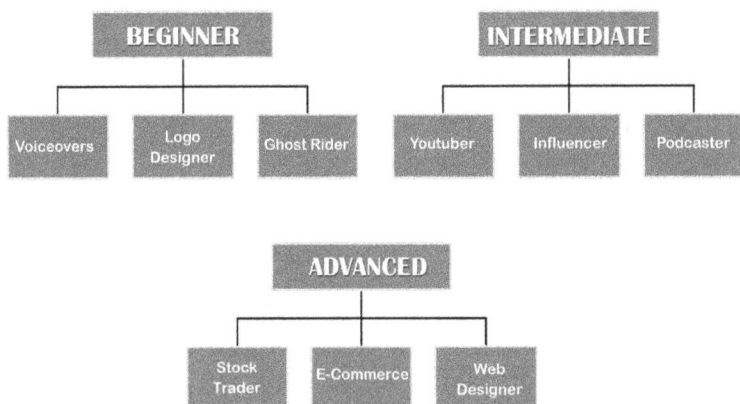

In reality anyone can do all three, but I made them in this order because I feel many don't know business and their first interaction with it is with this book.

I want to briefly mention something that to me is the most important thing in this book and which can be applied to life—and that is action. **Taking action is the decision maker on if you're going to get where you want to be or not. You can read all the books, go to every seminar, listen to all the tapes, and take notes all you want, but if you're not going to take action, then why even do any of that?** In reality, if you're not going to act upon your goal then it's just a waste of time. **"Multiple revenue streams are as important as having several necessary educators in life." ~Mike Jimenez (Founder of Radiotropolis and Oakmont Strategies).**

STATISTICS

I'm not going to focus a whole lot on this part of Chapter 4; however the reason I'm going to talk about the statistics is because I want to give you a chance to see what things you need to improve your revenue streams. It's always good to know how far you are from getting to where you want to be. In this case, how far you are from the revenue stream you need. How do you compare to a billionaire/millionaire on how much they make and how much you need to make for certain financial goals.

Although the statistics part of the chapter is small, it's important to know how much you need to make for your financial goals. This graph that you're about to read will tell you how much you need to make by minute, hour, day, week, month, year. Let's not waste any more time and let's instead get to the stats.

BREAKING DOWN
A MILLION DOLLARS

$1,000,000 / YEAR

$83,333 / MONTH

$19,230 / WEEK

$2,739 / DAY

$114 / HOUR

"It's all about PERSPECTIVE"

There you go, that's how much you need to make financially to reach $1million, $10million, $100million, $1billion, $10billion, $100billion, and, for fun,$1 trillion. Although this is all about the stats to reach financial goals, there's something that will help you get a better understanding on what's most likely going to happen each time you make more and more money. What happens if you want to go from making $50,000 a year to $1,000,000 and so forth? What a lot of people think happens, is you'll make little jumps of revenue coming in each week every week until you eventually reach your ultimate goal in the span of one year. For example, what people think will happen is that they'll make $960 as their average weekly amount before they start making bigger numbers.

The next week they'll make $1,000 (making only $40 more than the previous week). The week after that they'll make $1,100 making $100 more than the week prior to that. They keep on going week after week making little increases each week until the end of the year or whenever they want to make their goal ends up becoming true (aka, they think they're going to make money incrementally, or in little increases).

That could happen, however, it's most likely not going to happen like that. Instead what's most likely going to happen is they're going to make their money exponentially and or in big jumps. For example, what's going to happen is you'll go from making $1,000 a week to $5,000 the next month. The month after that you'll make $15,000 and the month after that you'll most likely make $40,000. After that month you'll make $100,000 and in the following months you'll make $400,000. Then, more and more as time goes on.

To put it simply, what's most likely going to happen is this. **Whatever your goal is in a year period, you're most likely not going to get there making little but consistent jumps each week throughout the whole year. Instead, you're most likely going to make small jumps in the first couple of months but after the sixth or eighth month, you're going to make 50 percent of the money. This happens when you compound your money. At first it doesn't seem like a lot, but after a couple of months pass you'll start to see the progress. After that point, just watch as the money grows exponentially.** By the way, this applies to anything, as long as you compound whatever it is you're doing, you'll see a huge increase of it at the end of the time you're doing it.

4 HUGE EXAMPLES

I'm going to talk about four of the biggest examples of companies which failed due to having either too many revenue streams or not enough revenue streams. One is going to talk about why having too many products was bad for a particular company and the rest of the examples are going to talk about why having a lot of revenue streams and products worked for three different companies. Keep in mind while reading this that this is one of many examples and I know that I'm already getting repetitive on examples, but this is an example for someone that has/is running a corporation or business. I promise I'm going to make this a good story in general for you, so don't worry. Plus, it's a good story.

I'm first going to talk about the reason having too many revenue streams is bad in some cases, then I'll get to why having not enough didn't work so well for some other companies. Apple is one of, if not the biggest, technology company there is in the world. They recently surpassed the trillion-dollar mark in human history! Not the first company to reach a trillion-dollar valuation, but it's still worth more than a trillion dollars as I speak. They sell a bunch of products, as you know, but you may be asking yourself what they have to do with why having too many revenue streams/products is bad for a company. Well, quite simply they almost went bankrupt because of it! "WHAT?" is what's going through your head right now, right? Well, let me explain.

After one of the founders of Apple, Steve Jobs got fired by his board of directors, Apple soon started to lose their value and sales went down almost every day. There were a bunch of reasons why they were failing--like outdated products, bad leadership, etc., but one of the biggest reasons why they failed, almost to the point of bankruptcy, was because they had too many products. You see, when a company has too many products that they sell, it usually causes their customers to question the company and what they're focused on, what is their main product, which than leads to confusion. In some cases, this works perfectly for a company. For example, grocery stores, malls, retail stores, etc., having various products works for them. They let their customers know that whenever they come into their store, they have a wide selection of products they can choose from which then leads to having a better chance of having something that the customer wants.

Again, this only works for retail stores, grocery stores, and malls, but even then, every one of those stores has a certain audience that they aim their products for. For Wal-Mart, their products are cheaper than most retail/ grocery stores, Wal-Mart is cheap and affordable for food and household items. Another example is Target. Target's products are almost always a bit more expensive and higher quality than a regular retail store like Wal-Mart, Ross, Pete's Market, etc. Target=higher quality food, appliances, toys, etc. than most stores. The last store I'm going to name is Ross. They focus on clothing that is affordable and that is off brand. Just like Target and Wal-Mart have their own types of products, Ross has off-brand and cheap clothes. Each store has their own type of products and they know who they sell to. Even stores that offer a huge variety of products have their own type of product and target customers.

Anyway, back to Apple. Once Jobs left and resigned as CEO, Apple though it would be a great idea if they offered more products. Products=more selection for people to buy from. So they started to sell scanners, printers, speakers, network servers, cameras, and a lot more. At first it worked fairly well, and some people liked it. Some didn't, but overall they were doing ok. So, what happened?

A couple years later they started selling more and more products, aka more computers; however, the problem was that almost every computer they sold at the time was outdated, was extremely expensive, and they released different versions of the same thing. They kept on going, more and more products that dipped in quality, the products weren't worth buying, and they weren't even what Apple at it's core was-a company that sold professional products to people that were quality products and that looked amazing.

The products they ended up selling also looked bad, with many people saying that they looked both ugly and not "Apple looking." It got so bad that they even started to sell video games! Yes, VIDEO GAMES. Comparing Apple from today and back then, you can easily see that they definitely weren't the same company. At the end of it, Apple had 350 products that they sold! It's crazy to think that the world's first trillion-dollar company that only sells a couple selected items used to sell over 350! That's another key point--why people had a hard time buying from Apple--because of their products and choice overload.

Choice overload is a cognitive process in which people

have a difficult time making a decision when faced with too many options. To help you understand choice overload better, and why it caused many people to stop buying from Apple, I'm going to give you a scenario/game that you can try on your friends.

On a beautiful hot summer day you decide to go to your local mall with your friends. In that mall there are two ice cream parlors. One has a huge selection of flavors that you can mix and match with each other. The other parlor only has three flavors, chocolate, vanilla, and strawberry. Quickly, I want you to set a timer for 15 seconds. In those 15 seconds you and whomever you're playing with has to choose one flavor out of the ones I'm going to give you but remember to time yourself. Your flavors are peanut butter, strawberry, cookie dough, cherry, pistachio, mint, rocky road, butter pecan, chocolate, hot fudge, vanilla, chocolate chip, coffee, cotton candy, and finally Neapolitan. Start the countdown. Do you have your answer yet? Unless if you're a very decisive person you'll most likely have a hard time picking one ice cream flavor from the 15 I gave you. After you eventually pick the flavor you want, it's time to go to the other parlor later in the day.

As you walk in you see below the countertop three flavors of ice cream that you can pick from; chocolate, vanilla, and strawberry. The same thing is going to happen however now your objective is to pick one of the three flavors that were offered to you in 15 seconds. Also remember to time yourself while you're at it. Ready, set go! Now 15 seconds passed by, how do you feel? Did you have an easier time picking what flavor you want, did you pick the flavor you want faster, or maybe you were able to pick your flavor almost immediately without hesitation. The whole point of this game was to show you that if given fewer options to a person, they'll have an easier time picking their answer. That's what happened to Apple.

Apple's regular, and loyal, customers were being bombarded by a bunch of products that looked the same and had little-to-no-difference between each other, to the point that they decided to go to another store that knew exactly why they were better than their competitor. On top of that, Apple's competitors didn't have the problem of having too many products. Apple's competitor's like IBM and Microsoft never gave their own customer too many options to decide from. Of course, there were other problems with Apple's products, such as being too complicated to use, not having enough storage space, easily breakable, etc., but this was the biggest one. Being bombarded by a bunch of different and complicated offers is one of the worst things you can do to your customers.

I want to mention this again because it's very important to know this: THIS DOSENT HAPPEN REGULARLY. Having too many products for companies is almost always in their favor because they know what they're doing and why they decided to add more products to their selection. In Apple's case, it happened because their products were ultimately really bad to use, and weren't worth buying. I also want you to remember that having too many products and having too many revenue streams are two completely different things. Having multiple revenue streams is never wrong to have for a company. In fact, this is what the whole chapter is about; you need a bunch of revenue streams. The wrong thing Apple did was that they had a bunch of products they sold that were no good. Again, products and revenue streams are two different things. REMEMBER THIS.

Ok, we got one of the four examples out of the way and now I'm going to talk about times having multiple revenue streams were good for a company's brand and their products themselves. These companies have a lot more types of revenue streams than most types of companies and I want to mention before we get any further that the companies I'm going to talk about are categorized on what they do. So instead of talking about one certain type of company, I'm going to talk about a bunch of companies that do the same thing, and that generally have more revenue streams than most companies do. Only one of the three types of companies I'm going to talk about is a single company and not a bunch of companies that do the same thing.

The first types of companies that I'm going to talk about are telecommunication companies and/or cellular providers. Verizon, AT&T, Sprint, T-Mobile, Cricket--what do they all have in common? They all offer a bunch of services, deals, phones, etc. Whatever provider you like or hate, they all get billions of dollars coming in each year. Even if they're the worst provider in the world, they get a huge cash flow coming in every single year. How do they do it? They have multiple revenue streams (and products) that they sell to their customers and get so much money from it! There are hundreds of reasons why TC's (telecommunication companies) are successful and make money, but the biggest reason why is because they have a bunch of ways to make money, aka revenue streams. TC's are smart because they know that once they get one customer hooked on their product, they know that they can push them into buying more and more products from them.

Think about your own TC, wither it's your own server, your parent's server, family, or whomever pays for it. I'm betting that you've heard them say that they have more products, services, deals, etc. for the person they're selling to. It's not only common in TC's but in-house services, car dealers, television companies, etc. The reason I'm bring this up is because this can help you in your own business/ company by helping make your revenue streams more successful. By that I don't mean that you should try to scam or make your customers a bad deal. What I mean is that you should get your salespeople or yourself to **get customers to buy better and more expensive products from you and not your competition. Always make sure that your customer keeps coming back to you.**

Again, I want to make it clear that you should have the

intension of helping your customers, and make sure when you up-sell your product that the product your selling is worth it, and that it will actually be useful for them. That's what the whole intention of being a salesperson is, and selling in general should be.

I wanted to quickly mention this because it's important to know and to use. TC's always make sure to have different services that they can sell to their customers, no matter what it ends up being. For example, one of the biggest TC's there is, Verizon, has hundreds of services that they offer to the public. One of the biggest ways that help them make money is by partnering up with technology companies (companies that sell phones, watches, tablets, computers, etc) to make their brand bigger, and to get more exposure. I'm sure you've heard ads on TV and apps that a certain type of TC is partnering up with a company who is selling the newest phone.

I'm betting that when you're on some type of app, TV channel, radio station, etc., you've heard some type of announcement that Verizon is offering the newest Galaxy phone. They offer you a free phone, accessory, watch, and so much more, but only if you switch with them. In 2019 alone, Verizon brought in $131.9 billion in revenue! Keep in mind that in 2019 they made multiple partnerships with Apple and offered their products that has a ton of revenue streams, but the lesson you should take away is that you should incorporate partnerships into your revenue streams and your business. Partnerships are great ways to get more exposure to your company. You can even take it as far as getting partnerships to help you create a new revenue stream. A couple ways to make new revenue streams out of partnerships is by creating a new products/service with the company you're partnering with.

Right now Wal-Mart and Shopify are partnering up to compete with Amazon. You can go more into detail on the deal, agreements, etc. but a quick recap is that Wal-Mart will now use Shopify's platform to expand their online marketplace. Wal-Mart is hoping that Shopify will help increase their monthly online users to double. On top of that, they're starting to let Shopify sellers to sell their products on Wal-Mart's marketplace. This is targeting Amazon for more competition. Whether this works out or not, one thing for sure is that both Wal-Mart and Shopify are going to get more people visiting their online business. Partnerships are great ways to get more people to notice your company and to grow your customer base.

The next type of companies that have multiple revenue streams, and are super successful with creating new ones, are film companies. Film companies have way more revenue streams than you think they have at first. Of course, the most obvious one is producing movies under their name (aka making money at the box office). However, they also use their movies to their advantage. They make toys/action figures based on characters of the films they make, they produce TV shows that go on different platforms like HBO, Netflix, Amazon Prime, etc. (again making partnerships are helpful to make your company grow), brand deals (for example Sony partnered up with Air Jordan to create shoes based on their movie Spiderman Into the Spider Verse), merchandise, product placement, amusement parks (Universal and Disney parks), novelization (movies turned into books), and games (board and app games).

As you read, you noticed that there's a bunch of different ways they make money. I just listed the main ways film companies make the most money/revenue streams but there's dozens of more ways. The movie theater company is a $136 billion-dollar business! When you were younger, or even now, have you've ever walked into your local Wal-Mart, Target, or even an online store and see that they're selling toys based on the newest movie at the time? I sure have. In fact, there's not only toys, but merchandise and accessories to the toys they're selling.

Right now they're selling millions of Star Wars toys to people, but when the series was at their peak (1978-1985), they sold more than 300 million action figures. 300 million toys were sold just because a bunch of kids loved a couple of space movies. Over the next 35 years they made the toy business into a 2-billion-dollar industry. And that was just a couple of movies; the total number of toys that were sold off each movie franchise is too much to count and is worth more than a couple of billion dollars.

This is only one revenue stream that the film company makes out of the dozens they have. To give you a quick estimate of how much one of the top film companies, Warner Media (owns Warner Brothers) made--$33.5 billion dollars in 2019 alone. There's so much money waiting to be made in the movie film business. This only one of many film companies that makes billions of dollars in revenue. The reason I chose the film company to talk about having many revenue streams instead of any other is that they're not only able to have multiple revenue streams, but because they're able to get so much free marketing without spending a dime. I know that almost all of the movie theater companies spend millions of dollars promoting their newest movie but some of them are smart enough to know that they don't need to spend millions of dollars on marketing.

I'm going to talk about the easiest way to get a attention to your company in Chapter 6 (marketing, advertising, and promoting), but here's a quick peek on what there is to come. One of the easiest ways to make money for your business, and is the reason I choose film companies, is by getting made fun of for whatever your selling. I know this sounds weird, but here's the reason why, and a little bit more into detail. What I should have said instead, to make it clearer, is to get meme's, trends, controversy, etc. made about your company. Again, I'm going to get more in detail about this in Chapter 6 but, for now, this is what I mean. When your company releases a new product and gets made fun of, (let's use a new movie for example) it's bound to get people to talk about it which than leads to buying it (to see if the rumors were true).

The newest Star Wars movie (Star Wars: The Rise of Skywalker) had a bunch of controversy--people said it was bad, that it sucked, and that it was the worst movie of all of the franchise. It was hated by almost everyone and anyone, however how much do you think that movie made in the box office? $1.075 billion! Disney made more than a billion dollars in the box office for a movie that almost everyone hated. **If it's popular enough that your neighbor knows about it, it has the potential to sell like pancakes.**

As you read, you could tell that film and movie companies have multiple revenue streams that make them billions of dollars each year. This is the second example of a type of company that used multiple revenue streams to their advantage and the lesson to be learned here as far as revenue streams, is this. **To create more revenue streams for your business is taking what you already have and adding on to it while being creative.** This works perfectly for movie companies and especially movie franchises that make movies that can be easily made into a new product. In Disney's case they used the franchise of Star Wars for the making of toys, clothing, merchandise, collectibles, etc. to create more revenue streams. They used something they already had and then they used it to their advantage to create more ways to milk as much money as they can off of it. This is one of the most important golden nuggets to learn from as far as Chapter 4 goes, and in this book, make sure you write it down and/or make sure to remember it.

The third and last type of company I'm going to talk about that mastered having multiple revenue streams is Alphabet. Although Alphabet isn't the first company you think of when asked which company has multiple and powerful revenue streams, it's true. Some of the companies Alphabet owns and operates are Android (the phone company), YouTube, Google, Double Click (helps for Google's advertisers), Google Drive, Google Play, Google Maps, Absence (web vendors for non-Google websites), and Google Chrome.

Here are some of Alphabet's main companies that bring them the most revenue out of all the ones they have. Although Alphabet's companies are huge and you most likely were surprised by the companies they own, here's some info on what they do. Alphabet is a company the founders of Google (Larry Page and Sergey Brin) created themselves. It serves as a hub for all the companies that Google currently owns, and the companies they purchased in the past. Alphabet has over 200 companies including Google itself, Ride, Gmail, reCaptcha, Tango, Now, Zagat, Wing, Life Science, and Inbox, along with many others. Although a lot of these company's sound made up, they're all owned by Alphabet Inc.

All 200 (and counting) companies that Alphabet owns

either serve as revenue streams for them directly or indirectly. For example, Gmail doesn't sell anything; instead they help Google gather information from their users. Gmail is a revenue stream that helps Alphabet make money indirectly. A company that does help Alphabet make money directly and that sells a product/service is YouTube. I, you, your grandma, and almost everyone uses YouTube, and in return they make a pretty penny each year. In 2019 alone they made $15 billion dollars, which is roughly 10 percent of what Google's total revenue was the same year.

Alphabet, the company itself, is a little complicated to get the full picture on, what they do, and how they relate to Google. I even had a hard time summarizing what they do while I was writing this. I explained it the best way I can, but if you want to get more info on what they do I encourage you to search for it on any platform/way you can. The golden nugget to learn from Google and their revenue streams is this. Revenue streams don't always have to sell a product or service itself to make your company grow. **Revenue streams could also be something that helps your company become more successful or grow in their customer service, product ideas, their website, marketing themselves, and so many other ways.** Find ways to make your company grow with and without selling a product/revenue stream.

So, after four examples and golden nuggets, you hopefully learned the importance of having multiple revenue streams for your business. Revenue streams come in all shapes and sizes, but the thing to remember is that no matter what revenue stream you come up with, it has to help either yourself or your company grow. If it doesn't, either let it go or figure out what's wrong with it. Next up is how and why you should invest in yourself.

INVEST IN YOURSELF

When the word "invest" comes up in a conversation, most people take it as a word of risk, loss, danger, stocks, etc. Especially if they've invested in something in the past and it didn't work out in their favor. However, investing in something could be practically anything and everything. You can invest in your business, your health, your love life, your house, your private life, your family, your education, in your city, your pets, and so much more. As you read, you can tell that you can invest into almost anything you want, even if it doesn't help you. Investing by definition means "devote one's time, effort, or energy to a particular undertaking with the expectation of a worthwhile result," which means you can invest into anything not just, for example, stocks, bonds, real estate, etc.

You've heard it all before, "You need to work-out and eat healthy to live a good life" or "You should go meditate and go clear you mind," and my favorite one is "The way you do one thing is how you do everything." Everything I mentioned you've heard someone say to you in one shape or form before and, YES, it's annoying at times. All these saying are common for parents, teachers, and whomever you grew up with when you were you were younger, or for some of the people reading this book, now. As you can guess, the reason why I bring these sayings up in the *"Invest in yourself"* part of the chapter is because I want you to know these are sayings that can help you in investing in yourself.

Before I go any further, I want you to know that I obviously don't know the situation you're in or how good or bad it is, so that doesn't give me the right to tell you what to do or not to do in your life. As far as business goes, I think I know some valuable things, but this is also why I don't want to make a huge deal of this part of the chapter. I'm not going to get into religion, politics, or on relationships because firstly these are subject that I don't know much about and secondly because these are subjects that you should keep to yourself. I'm just going to talk about the things that are simple and the things that anyone can do without having a hard time doing them. That being said, let's begin.

So, are those sayings helpful for investing in yourself, or not? Well, first we have to know what I'm talking about when I say you should invest in yourself. There are two subjects that I'm going to talk about in investing in you. The first subject I'm going to talk about is health. That includes physically and mentally. The second subject I'm going to talk about is investing in your goals. I'm pretty much going to talk about how to get closer to achieving your goals. These are the only subjects I'm going to talk about, health and your goals. In the case that you disagree with my advice to you, take whatever you can from it and learn from it--just one thing you can find and try to learn from it, or use it.

YOUR HEALTH

The first subject is health. Let's go back to the sayings you've heard before. Do they really help? Well in my opinion, and in the facts I'm going to talk about right know, yes, most of them are true and really do help you in investing in yourself. It all comes down to repetition. Take, for example, the experiment I talked about in Chapter 1. To refresh your mind, the experiment was to record yourself saying something both positive and negative. You would then record it and for half a month listen to the negative recording everyday for a couple minutes and the other half of the month listen to the recording of yourself that was positive. As time goes by and the more consistently you keep listening to the audio, you'll start to notice some changes in your behavior and the way you usually act.

This all happens because you started you day with a couple of minutes listening to positive/negative things. The more you start to hear and play the negative recording the more and more likely you'll start to behave/act negative. Same goes for the positive audio, if you start to listen to the positive audio, you'll most likely start to act more positively toward others. And it doesn't stop there; not only will your behavior change but your habits and the way you do thing normally will change as well. When I did this, I often found it difficult to keep focus and to do things I would have done normally. Even the simple things (keeping my things organized, doing the best I could while I was working on SAC, and even feeding my pets) were hard to do or I would do them carelessly.

Same thing would happen when I listened to the positive audio. I would have a more focused and better mindset while working on my business, keeping my things organized, and caring for my pets. Listening to the audio tapes both good and bad had a huge effect on everything I mentioned. I brought this up to show that the way you do one thing is more than likely going to be the way you do other things in your life, business, relationship, etc.

Although I do want to make it clear to you, and for everyone who's reading this, that this is not always true. In fact, this will not always happen to you or even frequently. The way to see results or to see any changes is by repetition. If you do a certain task that you do once or twice a week, the way you do that task is obviously not going to change the way you do everything else. However, if you do the task consistently and try to adapt the way you do the task on other things you'll start to change quickly.

It might sound confusing to some of you, but in simple words it is this. **The way you do one task is not always the**

way you're going to do everything else; the trick is to adapt the way you do one task into every other task you want to change while being repetitive. You might have to read that a couple of times to fully understand it, but once you do, you'll be one step closer to investing in yourself. The reason I brought this up in the investing in you part of the chapter is because one of the biggest ways to invest in yourself is by changing the way you do most things for the better. I already talked a lot about habits and how to change them in Chapter 1 if you want to read about them again.

YOUR PHYSICAL WELLBEING

The next thing I want to talk about is investing in yourself physically. I know this is going to get a bunch of people mad or offended when talking about working out and about their health, so if any of that offends you go ahead and skip to the begining of the next section. This isn't going to be talked about too much in this book, but when talking in investing in yourself this topic is bound to be talked about.

Investing in yourself consists of getting things that will help you improve in your life and goals. You obviously want to be able to live life to the max and experience everything that brings you joy. For you it might be skydiving, racing sport cars, having a nice house, hiking, bungee jumping, and whatever else it might be, we can agree that you want to live to be able to do the thing that bring you joy. The thing is, a lot of the things you want to do in your life may require you to do some physical activity, unless it's online playing, but besides that you're most likely going to have to be active. That's why you want to be somewhat fit or not overweight. You want to be able to do things you want without worrying about how much it cost or about your weight. If you're overweight or fat you won't be able to do the things you want easily.

I'm not in your situation, but one thing I can say is that I'm sure you don't want to be fat or overweight. This is why I'm going to talk about the specifics on what to do to become fit. All I'm going to do is tell you a couple of ways to become fit and exercises you can do from home or at a gym. I'm not going to talk about diets or the food you should eat too much because I don't know the situation you're in. These are

100 Jumping jacks every 2 minutes, 5 times, resting period 15 sec.

Run a mile in 10 mts. Gradually increase by 1 min until you run it in 6 mts. Resting period 10 mts.

Ride for 30-60 minutes, 3 to 5 days a week

5 Sets, 5 Times, resting period = 90 sec.

all just workouts and diets that anyone that's a healthy and normal person can do. I encourage you to fit the workouts to your liking. I'm going to talk about to the way that fits you, so that it's better for you. Yes, these are facts from people who do this professionally and who have done it before so don't @ me.

The first thing I'm going to talk about is workouts, specifically leg workouts. Here's a list of some of the best workouts you can do with a couple of dumbbells, weights, or without any equipment needed.

Investing in you is a step to creating success. When I say invest in yourself, I don't mean buying a bunch of designer wear or buying a new car. No, when I say invest in yourself, I mean learning something new that can improve yourself, listing to audio books, working out, go to a seminar, etc. Investing in yourself means to improve yourself and your skill for the better. It could be as easy as skipping a McDonalds for lunch. For example, if you're into a team such as basketball, you can invest in yourself by staying after a game and practicing. If you want to lose weight, then invest in yourself by getting a work-out set and take action working out.

YOUR GOALS

The second thing I'm going to talk about to invest in yourself is investing in your goals. A little info before I talk about how to invest in your goals and how to have a better chance of accomplishing them. All the strategies I'm going to talk about to achieve your goals should be used on big or challenging goals, instead of little or easy ones.

For example, when I refer to your goals I don't want you to think about making your bed or little things you need to do because they aren't really urgent goals. Instead, they're tasks and although accomplishing your own tasks are important, they aren't something that's important to finish. In the next and last part of the chapter (time), I'm going to talk about why doing little tasks are costing you thousands of dollars daily. So, for now, don't worry about little things you need to do when thinking about your goals. This is all about your goals that are challenging or that are truly important. That being said, let's start.

There are three things you need to keep in mind and apply every time you want to achieve a goal of yours. CBDA is the "formula" you need to use every time you want to accomplish any goal of yours. CBDA is to be the best way to accomplish every/any goal. I use it whenever I have goal, like writing this book. I learned that writing a book takes a bunch of patience and time to complete and at the start of writing this, I struggled a lot in the middle of the school year which required a lot of my time. I also couldn't believe I had to write over 150 pages worth of content in a couple of months' time. It was a huge goal to accomplish at the time, and even as I'm writing this. However, around Chapter 3 I've learned one of the best ways/methods to accomplish my goals and by far the best I've ever used.

Crystallize, Break Down, and Apply/Act; that's what each of the letter CBDA stand for otherwise the best way to accomplish your goals. Let's break it down and see what they all mean and the steps. First off, Crystallize. To crystallize your goals means to make your goal crystal clear. In other words, make sure you know exactly what you want from your goal and to make you know what's going to become the outcome of it. All crystallizing is (as far as goals go) is making sure what your goal is and to make sure it's truly what you want. Immerse yourself in that goal and picture yourself achieving it.

For example, let's use buying your dream house for your goal, (every example I'm going to use, I'm going to refer back to buying your dream house) when you made the decision of buying your dream house, the first goal is crystallize it. What would you do? You would make sure that house you want is 100 percent the house you want, make sure you looked at the pictures of your rooms and bathrooms, even visit the house yourself if you can, just to get a better understanding of the house. Just like Dan Pena would do, "Smell the leather." He would go to the Rolls-Royce dealership, go inside one of their cars, and smell the leather of the new car.

He'd make sure he was so focused on his goal that he would go as far as physically touching it. If that's what you need to do then go ahead and do it. In this case, go as far as going inside and getting a tour of the house, even if you're not able to buy it yet. That's what crystallizing you goal is. Making sure you know exactly what you goal is, imaging yourself achieving that goal, and even going as far as physically touching it (if that's possible). Hopefully you understood what crystallizing your goals/the first part on achieving your goal.

The next part on achieving your goal is Breaking Down. Breaking down your goal is the most important part to achieve your goal besides the A part of your goal. It's self-explanatory, you need to break down your goal into steps and parts to achieve it. Although there's a little more to it than just breaking it down, let me further explain. The way to break down your goals is by doing it in segments, preferably 10-20 parts; however, you need to do it backwards. For example, this is how I would do it.

Firstly, I'd see myself moving into the house and buying all the furniture, choosing where the piano would go, what room would be mine, maybe getting ready to paint the house, etc. The second thing I would break down would be giving the signature to the house and giving the realtor the check for it. Then the next step would be seeing me calling the homeowner and saying I was going to purchase the house. The step after would be getting the news that I finally got the money I needed to generate from my business to purchase the house. Then I'd see myself getting a huge contract for my business that would make tons of money.

The next step would be building my business up and getting more and more clients over time. After that step I'd see myself facing all the struggles and challenges that comes with building my business up, laying some of my employees off, and maybe seeing my business almost going bankrupt. I'd have a couple more steps that required challenges, struggles, ups and down but that's the gist of it.

That's what breaking down your goal is, seeing what your goal is from achieving/accomplishing it all the way down to starting to begin it. The reason this is so useful when working towards your goals is because it shows yourself the steps you need to take form begging to end. Obviously, the way you're going to imagine it isn't how it's going to be 100 percent, but I'm guessing it's going to be somewhat what you've pictured. This step of achieving your goals allows you to have a good picture on what you're going to go through when achieving your goals.

Again, this can be used for any goal you have. If buying your dream car is your goal, great! The first step would be driving the car out of the dealership. The next step would be driving to the dealership to get the car. The next step would be getting enough money from your business to by the car. Next would be building your business up, and so forth. This is the most important part of CBDA besides A; make sure you do this step because without it you'll be lost. Just remember to break down your steps backwards/from the end to beginning. Great, you got 2/3 of the steps to achieve your goals done!

What else is there? The next and final step to achieving your goals is to Apply/Act.

PUT IT ALL TOGETHER

The last step to making your goals into a reality is to act and apply steps one and two to your goals. Although that sounded obvious and simple, it's actually way harder to do than any other step previously. Without this step you're nowhere and you'll make the other two steps useless. I know I've mentioned this time and time again but it's true, YOU NEED TO ACT ON EVERYTHING YOU DO! Most people get steps one and two right and actually get it done perfectly. However, when they get to the last and final step, they don't get any further. This is the hardest and most challenging step to do, even for me. I'm sounding repetitive, I know, but I can't stress enough the last and final step to achieving your goals.

We finally went over three things you need to do to invest in yourself mentally, physically, and in your goals. Hopefully you learned a little more now in investing in your goals than you did before you started. Remember to always act and actually do your goal instead of just imagining and dreaming about it. Next it's time for one of the most important things to talk about in the whole book! Get ready for a lot more golden nuggets coming at your face, because what's coming up is full of them!

TIME!

As I mentioned in almost every chapter, one way or another, I always find myself talking about your time and how it's your most valuable asset. Truth be told, I can easily make a whole book dedicated all about the value of your time and how you can use it to the max! So, I think it's fair enough to go a little more into detail about how you can use your time more efficiently and how successful people look at time. I'm going to show you why doing simple tasks like cleaning your room or going to the supermarket cost's you hundreds, if not thousands, of dollars.

The question is, "How can you use your time more efficiently?" It all comes down to the things you do yourself. What do you do each day that is either not worth doing, or something that takes up time that can be used for a better purpose, like working towards your goal. For a lot of you reading this book I'm guessing there's dozens of things that you do that isn't worth your time, or that can be used for something else more productive.

For example, cleaning. Whether you clean your room, your house, or anything that takes up your time, I'm guessing it takes about an hour to do, right? Whatever or however long it takes for you to clean something, you could've used that time for something else that's actually more productive like working on your goals, reading, working on your business, or even doing something that makes you happy. The question still lies, how can you use your time more effetely while still completing your daily tasks? **Look at another solution that allows you to work on your goals or whatever you want to actually do while still getting your other daily tasks done.** Let me explain.

When you do a task that isn't working towards your goal (or something that you want to do) you automatically think that you can only do one thing or another. So, as a result, you don't see any other options or solutions to fix your problem. That's the part that you need to figure out yourself, depending on your situation. I'll give you some solutions in a couple of paragraphs. All of the talk about time leads me to my next point which is, how do successful/wealthy people think of their time and why doing simple task's every week is costing you hundreds if not thousands of dollars? I can explain this in one easy example that almost anyone can relate to.

Let's say that your goal for the end of the year is $1,000,000. Just like anything, you want to see how much your goal (in this case making $1,000,000) will cost every day, week, month, etc. Doing some math, the goal of a $1,000,000 consists of you making around $115 an hour. Keep that in mind for now.

Think to yourself, how long does it take you to do all your daily tasks and activities? Like showering, getting ready for your day, eating your three meals, driving to work or school, checking your phone, showering again perhaps, talking to family, working on your business, etc. I could go on forever, but let's use the daily amount of time you're on your phone each week. The average person uses their phone about three hours, more or less, a day. If you convert into weeks that's 21 hours each week that's spent on your phone.

Back to the point; remember how much you need to make each hour to make $1,000,000 a year? $115 each hour. Take that $115 and multiplying it by how long you spend on your phone each week (21) it adds up to $2,415. Each week your phone costs you $2,415, did you ever think about that? If you break it down, it costs you $350 each day to use your phone! What's the point of this? The point is that your time, and how you use it, is the most important thing you have, so try to use it only for important things you need to do, not little things like cleaning your room or cleaning your house.

I want to go back to when I said I'll give you some solutions to make little things or tasks stop taking up your time. Let's get the obvious ways first. Cleaning your room the day before, making your bed in the morning, paying or bribing (whatever works for you) a younger or older sibling to do your tasks, having a roommate clean your stuff in return for money or something, or not doing it at all, if it's not that urgent, etc. Those are the main ways you can make your little tasks go away or fix themselves, so what's the best or key thing to do to keep your tasks from taking up your time?

The key is creativity. It's true. Creativity is the key to stop little things from taking up your time. What I mean by that is that you need to look at your situation and find a solution to your problem. That's where the creativity part comes in, you need to become creative and see a bunch of solutions that a normal person wouldn't come up with. Be creative with it! Some of you might even go as far as asking your neighbor to do the tasks for you. Have an open mind and figure out what's going to work for you in your situation.

That's what I'm going to leave you with. Be creative, both creative and open minded with your answers/solutions to your problem.

YES! You're about to go into Chapter 5! The next chapter is going to talk about a lot of different approaches for your business to make it grow and thrive. However, there is also a part of the chapter that will explain three main keys that will make any type of business, organization, non-profit, etc. become extremely successful and profitable. Get ready and begin to read the many ways to make your business grow!

CHAPTER FIVE

MANY METHODS TO MAKE YOUR BUSINESS SUCCESSFUL (AND THREE GOLDEN KEYS FOR ANY BUSINESS)

"Just because you're a CEO, don't think you have landed. You must continually increase your learning, the way you think, and the way you approach your organization"

~Ursula Burns

———————

SACRIFICES ARE NEEDED

As you and many others reading this know, sacrifices are made for everything you want, big or small. The truth is **that many of you don't want to make sacrifices to get what you want. In a lot of other cases, many of you are ready to make sacrifices, but when you're on the spot and you're needed to make sacrifices in your business, life, goals, etc., you back out in the last minute.** Although right now you might think to yourself that you're ready for the challenges and sacrifices, you'll never know until you're on the spot and are about to do it.

Anyway, I'm going to start talking about some facts and harsh truths about having a business to give you an idea about what's really going to happen to you when you're actually in the business and starting to struggle. There's absolutely no question about it, you need to see the reality of owning a business. That's where most people stop wanting to start or run a business, whether it's a startup or an already-owned business. They don't know how to manage the risk they're going to have to take, and are afraid that they'll lose everything they put into their business, which then leads them to the belief that he/she shouldn't invest in their own company.

Did you know over 20 percent of business fail in their very first year? Since there are 627,000 new businesses created every year, that means 125,000 businesses fail each year. Think about it. If you and four other friends start new

new businesses, at least one of you guys is guaranteed to fail in your first year alone. Let's take it further and let's see how many businesses fail further along the line. In the first five years of starting a business, 50 percent of them fail. Now that number can fluctuate, but also put that in perspective. Going back to those four friends that you picked, let's add five more friends to the list, including you. You guys are five years into your business and all of a sudden five more friends and their businesses fail. Although I'm saying five of *your friends* fail, there's also pretty big chance you're going to fail along with them.

How does this contribute to the sacrifices you're going to make? Well, if you're not rethinking starting a business yet, it's good to know now that if you don't want to become one of the businesses that fail in the first five years, you need to start making sacrifices as soon as you start. You're going to be willing to get sleepless nights, harsh words from critics, lay off your employees, etc. Sacrifices also require you to start diluting your free time, and instead, dedicate it to your business. The biggest one of all, you need to actually be in the business.

Thousands of people who own or operate a business aren't even at the business and are doing other things instead. It doesn't only happen with new business but also with big corporations that are hugely known. They either don't physically operate the business or aren't dedicated to it. It's not bad to de-stress and do things you want to do, that make you happy, instead of working on your business. However, if you want better results and a higher chance of succeeding, you're going to want to spend more time on it than most people do.

WORK SMARTER OR HARDER?

Should you work smarter or harder, this is the question that almost everyone argues on and although the easy and most common answer out of the two answers is working smarter instead of harder, let's take a deeper look into it. To look into it, let's look at the pros and cons of both answers. Before we go into it, I want you to take a second to think

	SMARTER	HARDER
TIME	✓	✗
ACTION	✗	✓
PHYSICAL	✗	✓
IMMEDIATE RESULTS	✗	✓
LONG-TERM RESULTS	✓	✗

about your own answer.

Now that you looked through each pro and con of working harder and smarter what's your conclusion? Whatever it may be and whatever reasons you have that makes you believe that one's better than the other, here's the best answer to the million-dollar question, "Should you work harder or smarter?" Why not both? You didn't expect that did you? Yes, I know that that's not what everyone wants to hear. However, the thing is that most people don't want to pick both and are certain that they have only one option when in reality they could pick both and have time to do it.

Think about yourself and a time when you were confronted with the question. Here's what you most likely did, one of three things. One, you picked either working smarter instead of harder or vice versa. Two, you chose to brush it off and not do either, or three, you chose to do both. I'm sure that you only did option one or two and didn't choose three. The reason most people don't pick option three, and most likely pick option's one and two is because they either feel pressured by themselves or by someone else to pick one of working harder or smarter, they couldn't choose between working harder and smarter, they felt that it was too hard to do both at the same time, it felt undoable to do both, or they decided to scrap the idea and do none of the options.

I personally did both options one and two before even getting close to picking option three many times before.

Why? Because of all of the options I've mentioned, it was too hard to choose between the two of working harder or smarter. I didn't think it was possible to do both at the same time, and I decided to scrap the idea all together. This happens to millions of business owners all over the world. The question is, how can you do both at the same time successfully? I want to quickly mention that the reason I didn't say how to do easily or without stress is because you're guaranteed to encounter both stress and difficulties along the way. That being said, here's what to do to become successful at it.

BE DIFFERENT

Here's one of the hardest things to do in a business, but one of the most important things to do also. Being different is something everyone has/had a hard time doing. This includes me, local businesses, mom and pop shops, the biggest companies in the world, the most profitable companies in the world, and even the most successful people in the world went through this. This is something that requires you to think of things you thought you could never come up with, changing your business structure, doing a lot of research on new things that can make you different, and things that almost no one has ever done or thought of doing before.

Although it's super easy for some people to do, they can come up with a bunch of different solutions and different things you can do in hours, if not minutes or seconds, but for the majority of people, including myself, it's really hard to do. After many people start to find and search up ways to differentiate themselves and their business from their competition, they come to the realization that's it's really hard to do and it takes a lot of time. Ultimately, they end up forgetting about it and keep doing what they're doing. They don't innovate their company to become different and become more appealing to their customers.

Although it's sad, it's the truth. Many people don't become different because it's too hard to do. Here's another thing that most people don't do either. This surprisingly doesn't really happen to small businesses but instead to big corporations and or hugely successful companies who "made it." So, how can you become different than you are now, and become better than your competitors, to get them out of business?

In any business you have many things to consider when you want to stand out from your competitors, depending on what type of business you have. However, just like any business, there's also key principles you can apply which will make you stand out from your competition. What are they? Customer experience, great/better distinguished products, and have what they lack. Those are three key elements to differentiate from your competition in almost any area of business that if used they will make you stand out.

Let's dig deeper. Let's start with the first thing to make

yourself stand out and to make yourself different from your competitors; great customer service. You know it, I know it, Bill Gates knows it, and every big business knows it; service is extremely important to a business of any size, big or small. You've seen videos of people on YouTube, Instagram, Facebook, etc., of people going to stores and asking for the manager's numbers most likely because of the horrible customer service that they had. Here's a perfect example, let's say you walked in a store that sells jewelry and at the time you're looking to engage to your significant one with a ring! You look for the best ring that's there (at least one that you can afford).

As soon as you walk into the store the first thing you notice is that nobody is asking you how they can help you, if you have any questions, and no one's paying attention to you. I don't know about you but that never happens to me or anyone I see walk into a jewelry store. As I walk in, I get greeted and taken care of, even if they know that I'm not going to buy anything. You brush it off thinking everyone's busy. You start to look at their selection of rings, and ask the employees about them--what's the best one to get for the price, quality, where it comes from, etc.

As you're asking the questions, the employee's answering them while getting annoyed with you, and although he's not telling you, it's clear and obvious that he is. On top of that, he's not even answering your question; instead, he changes the subject and tells you that he needs to help another customer. Still, you think that there are probably a lot of people that need help outside the store or maybe the employee needed to clean up or something. He walks away and instead of helping another customer or cleaning the store, he goes in the back of the store and uses his phone instead.

What have you done? NOTHING! In the whole time you've been there, not once have you been rude to them, you're not yelling at them, everything is calm, etc., but even then he's still annoyed with you. Do you still think that they're the best option for you if they're not caring about you and your needs? If it were me, I'd walk out as soon as I could. Anyway, if you haven't walked out already, you're debating buying a ring from them now, after both you and the employee are annoyed.

Do you honestly believe that you're going to buy their best ring after nobody's caring about you, you've been getting annoyed, etc.? To summarize it all up, do you think you're going to tell people that the best place to go to buy a ring, necklaces, or any jewelry is from them? I don't think so. Now, you're back at the point where the employee left you unattended. You're really starting to get annoyed, and you're getting ready to leave.

After 10 minutes go by, and he gets back to you, he finally comes to the question, "Which ring do you want?" Are you going to still buy from them after all you've been through, or are you going to go to another store?

The next option you have is to go to another store. Although it's a little more expensive than the store you just went to, you give it a shot. As soon as you walk in the store, the first thing that you see is an employee walking up to you and asking if they can help you with anything. That's already one better thing than what you went through with the other store. You start asking questions about certain rings just for the heck of it, and the employee is answering each and every question you asked him. The employee is giving you suggestions on rings that would suit you, better options on the price, etc. Most importantly, you're clearly having a way better time than the first store you went to. Then the question finally comes up, "Which ring would you want?" Let's see what happened so far.

You've gotten sold on a beautiful ring for you and your partner, you've gotten amazing customer service, you notice that whenever you had a question the employee is answering each of them with an easy and clear answer. You have the money to buy this beautiful ring in front of you and although it's a little more expensive than the first store you went to, it's worth every penny. What would you do? Say yes or no? I think I can clearly say openly that you're going to buy that beautiful ring for your future partner.

Why is this, because you've had a way batter customer experience than any other store you went to? At first, you would've bought from the first store you went to because of the price, but because you got horrible customer service you decided to go to the other store, even if it's a bit more expensive. This is why customer service is something that is clearly advantageous and can make a potential customer pick you over your competitor.

Let's say that you're still not convinced on buying from the second and better store because you still want to get a cheaper ring than the ring you just saw, and you don't really care about customer service so you go back to the first store after all. As you say thank you to the second store you start to walk out and ready to go the first store saying that the price is still better. Just as you're about to walk out something stops you dead in your tracks. You see in the corner of your eye a beautiful ring embedded with diamonds that's perfect for your significant other.

The next thing you know you're looking at the ring and asking questions about it. You soak up all the information of the ring and you can't take your eyes of off it. You say to yourself "I NEED THAT RING," and finally ask the question, how much does the ring cost? Just as expected, it costs WAY more than the other two rings combined. Don't forget, you still want to get the ring that's inside your price range.

You think about it for a couple seconds and finally come to conclusion that you HAVE to buy the ring. It would be crazy if you didn't buy it. Yes, it's way out of your price range, but for starters, the ring isn't like any other ring you've seen before in your life, you're going to have a ring that most people aren't going to have, and a wedding ring that your partner is going to LOVE. Best of all, and the cherry on top, all of the times that you've been at the store you've gotten compliments, advice on the best ring for you, everyone's been kind; they're customer service was amazing! With everything being said, do you want to buy the ring or not? I'm guessing that you most likely said "OF COURSE!"

This all happened because of what? **The customer service and the amazing ring that almost every other jewelry store doesn't have. In other words; the customer service was amazing, the stores product was amazing, and they had something (in this case a ring) that every other store didn't have. If you have all three things in your favor, you'll have a way higher chance of getting picked than your competitor.**

DON'T BE STUCK IN THE SMALL PHASE

Remember earlier when I said that you have to change in the beginning of the book? Well, all the things I wrote about were mainly when you start or in the early stage of starting a business. Hopefully you overcame all the challenges that you faced in starting your business, but now we're in the middle stage of growing your business, and this is something that everyone encounters in their business--they're stuck in the small phase of their business and decide not to grow it anymore. In many cases that not a problem, some people just want to be in the business of being small, they want to be secure in money, they want to be able to pay their bills without a problem, and to have more money saved up or able to go on more vacations, etc.

For a lot of people, it's what makes them happy and they feel accomplished. Personally, I don't want to do that. I want to have my company building, I want to be in the Fortune 500 top companies, and I want my company and me to be known all over, throughout the world. But for a lot of people they're satisfied with what they have, and want to stay at that level, which is fine and it's what works for them. For those of you reading this that want to be in the type of small business phase you can go to and read the next part of the chapter because I'm going to talk all about how to grow your businesses out of the small business phase.

You need more people!!! This is the key when talking about how to get you out of the small business phase. It's self-explanatory. More people and innovative employees/ partners = bigger business. This is the basic and most effective way to grow your business. I want to emphasize the fact that this is the way to *grow your business*. Growing your business doesn't always mean that it's going to be profitable. I'm going to talk about more examples of why growing too big without being careful at a fast rate can be bad for both the business and the owner.

This won't happen too often since this mainly happens with franchisees. Getting back to the point, why do you need more people to grow, even if you have a scalable operation without the need of employees, marketers, a board, etc.? The reason you need more employees, partners, ideas, etc. is because the more of them you have, the more of a chance that you're going to be able to get more ideas on how to expand and grow your business through whatever challenge you have.

You've heard the phrase before, "two heads are better than one," right? Well, it's true in almost anything you do, including business. For example, say you want to expand to a bigger audience that's going to want your products. You personally can't think of a solution. What do you think is going to happen if you get more people to help you come up with a solution to the problems your business has at the moment? You're going to get different answers to it.

This applies to sales, customer service, marketing, etc. The more people you get to help you, the more chances you're going to come up with an amazing solution to the problem you had. That's where your board comes in, your board helps you get ideas on how you can get the solution to the business problem. That's also why you want to hire people who are innovative and smart in your area of business.

This is something really important to know, because, yes, you can hire a bunch of people who can come up with solutions to the problems you have, but all the answers they give you can be horrible. Imagine if you go as far as applying the solution that you thought was going to be amazing but instead it fails, and now you're going to have to look at what happened that was wrong. You need to find people who know the type of business.

Think about it this way. If you're a basketball player that wants to get good at guarding who are you going to ask for help; Michael Jordan, the best basketball player ever or a barber down the street? You're going to ask MJ to help you with dribbling, three pointers, dunking, etc. Now here's another scenario, say you want to get the best hair cut possible, you have two options; you can ask MJ for help or the best barber on the world that's been cutting hair for years and years? You're going ask for the best barber to cut your hair, why? Because that's his area of expertise, it's not in basketball or anything else. You want to find out what you need help with, and who the best person for the job is.

If you really want to pinpoint the perfect person to help you with your problems, you need to find exactly what they've done in the past. It's like saying you're good at every single thing about basketball, but you suck at only one thing, rebounds. You have two choices; you can go with Michael Jordan (which is already a great option) or you can pick Dennis Rodman, the best rebounder of the Bulls team and one of the best ones ever. Who would you pick? If you don't know what each of their abilities or you're not from Chicago, you'll have a hard time picking the person to help you with. However, if you do your research and figure out exactly what their record is, you'll know that you should pick Rodman.

In other words, **know what person you want to get help from based on the problem or challenge you have; if you don't, you'll have a bunch of people helping you like headless chickens.** What's the whole point of this part of the chapter? If you want to get out of the small phase in business, you want to hire more people that can help you grow. However, you want to make sure that the people you're getting help from is going to give you the best advice in the problem you have. Make sure they're already having a great experience on what you're going to ask them for help with. If you don't, it's going to be like asking a legless man how to win the 100-meter Olympic race.

DON'T BE SCARED TO CHANGE

Change is scary isn't it? For a lot people it is, and especially if they have to change their business, it's even scarier because they don't know if they're going to succeed. For a lot of people, if they don't succeed in whatever change they did, they'll be out of business or worst case scenario, they'll go into debt that they can't pay.

Think about it yourself, have you've ever made a change to your business or even in your personal life that was scary, and you had a chance that you could've been horribly wrong. How about in your businesses or whatever you were hoping to succeed, but ultimately failed in? I'm betting everything I have that you had many things that you thought were going to work extremely well, or that you think wouldn't fail horribly.

Once you did whatever you thought would work, that was a big change to your businesses, you realized that it wasn't such a great idea and ended up failing. That's exactly what keeps people from changing their business for the better. Have you ever had ideas that you thought were amazing and just before you were going to go through with it you decided not to because of a past experiences you had? I've for sure had great business ideas that I didn't do that now, looking at it, could've been one of the best things that could've happened for my business.

This is something that's commonly feared and not thought about in a good way. **However, change is something that's needed in running a business or at the least making it successful. You, I, huge companies, etc. need to be willing to change, big or small, for the better.** A personal story for change that I went through is SAC (Smiles Against Cancer). After we had so many things planned for our third year in business, we got hit by the virus which in turn made us stop all of the things we had planned for the third year, so we decided to plan and strategize for the future.

I was thinking on things that could help us to grow our word out for the next year while my dad (partner of SAC) was also thinking of ways we could grow our business. After a couple hours my dad came up with the idea of reaching out to different problems in our world other than cancer.

He explained to me that if we were to reach out to different types of problems and diseases we would be able to reach out to not only the child cancer community, but to people who believe and support other types of problems, like global warming, diabetes, ADHD, etc. Immediately I was opposed to the idea. Can you guess why?

Because I didn't want to change, I didn't want to change SAC and reach out to different problems in our world because I thought that helping kids that have cancer is all we did (because we did), but I didn't realize that if we were to change and do the plan that my dad said we would be able to reach out to millions of more people that support different challenges in our world, we would help those in need that are battling other diseases or problems in our world, and the biggest one of all--we would be able to grow and expand to different communities.

This happened a couple months ago, about the time I was writing chapters two and three. As I said earlier at the book, I'm learning new things as I'm writing this book which made me realize that changing is hugely important to do in running a business and in my personal life. After I realized, I planned to talk about it in this chapter.

Since then we're still in quarantine, we still can't do much in SAC, and we can't implement the new ideas that we came up with. However, my dad and I came upon something that will help SAC grow hugely once we're able to reopen our organization, and all because I was willing to change.

Another huge example of a company that was willing to change their business is happening right now as I'm writing this! You may or may not know of the company, Kodak. They were a company that's sole purpose was to sell camera equipment, cameras themselves, etc. They were huge in the 80s and 90s, and one of the most successful companies at the time. They grew experientially and were the number one camera company in the world at one point. However, after their best point of existing they slowly started to decline in sales, customers, etc. It got to the point where they declared bankruptcy in 2011.

They still existed and came out of bankruptcy, but they were never able to go back to the point where they were originally at. This happened because of new phone companies that were able to incorporate cameras into their phone, and their quality was just as good, if not better, than the quality that Kodak had. This sounds like a bad story to tell for being able to change right? In fact, the reason they went bankrupt was because they were able to able to innovate and change their business. However in all, something that Kodak still had their factories and the space to build whatever they wanted to whether it would be cameras or not.

In 2020, and actually just a couple weeks prior to me writing this, they got a HUGE contract from the American government to find a vaccine for the corona virus. WHAT you may be saying. How can a camera company get a huge contract from the government to build a vaccine for the public? Everyone thinks that right now. They're getting criticism left and right, and a lot of it isn't pretty.

Regardless of what people think of them, Kodak was able to get a contract from the government, and it got them a pretty penny for it. However, why was this able to happen? Because they were able to change industries. Let's face it, who's going to buy a separate camera from a company when they have a camera just as good, if not better, in their pocket. NOBODY, unless it's for big projects like filming a movie. Kodak realized this, saw what they had in their resources, and said were going to change our company.

A little insight on this, as I mentioned before. Kodak had a huge factory that had enough space to build whatever they wanted to. They also had the machinery to do it. They saw what they had and decided they were going to do something about it which then led them to go into the medical business and try to build a vaccine for the government. They had the equipment, they had the building, and they had the space, so they decided to go with it (in other words, they were able to change to the medical company because it was going to become easy to do if they had nothing).

Again, I want to mention that this happened literally a couple weeks ago and they're in the process of finding a vaccine as I'm writing this. They were willing to change their whole company and now they have a fresh new start! Even if they don't find the vaccine before the completion, they still have the equipment to stay in the medical industry!

The last company I want to talk about changing is, surprisingly, 7/11. In case you live under a rock, 7/11 is a convenience and gasoline store. One thing that I found crazy is that they have more locations than McDonalds, which is more than 70k stores compared to McDonalds, which is 38k. What is even more crazy is that the comparison is based worldwide!

How is this related to changing your business and industries you're asking? Being a convenience/gas store is a simple enough industry, right? Well, the way they started is a lot different than what they are now. Originally, they were an ice company that wasn't even interested in doing any convenience store, because back than there weren't any.

Back then a **convenience** store wasn't really a convenience store, because back then you would have to go to a full-on grocery store that was always busy and that almost always was farther away than you would want it to be--it wasn't convenient. In addition, they were already pretty successful as an ice company. They weren't making ridiculous amounts of money, but they were doing alright.

They eventually were pitched an idea by Jefferson Green about a mini grocery store that offered simple things like snacks, drinks, and the essentials someone needed.

They went through with the idea and opened their first ever convenience store. It still wasn't named 7/11, but it was thought of as the first ever convenience store. They didn't want to make it the biggest part of the business, so they just opened to get some extra revenue every month. However, they soon came to the realization that they could make a lot more money if they were to open up a couple of extra stores and possibly franchise them.

Still focused on the ice side of the business, they opened another store. When they opened that, it was almost identical to the first one they originally opened. Soon enough, the second store was also doing great, so in response they opened yet another store, and another, and another. Soon they had opened dozens of stores and completely went with the idea of shifting their business to convenience stores! They've had their ups and downs since then, but eventually they grew it large enough to the point of having more stores, worldwide, than McDonalds! Remember, they were originally an ice company and didn't want anything to do with being a convenience store.

Change is something every company owner and company has to be able to accept. Although at times it could fail for them, there's also going to be many uphill battles. Change is neither good nor bad, it's just a trial and error game; however, you'll have a better chance of succeeding if you do your research, have a product that will apply to your customers, and if you make sure that the change will truly help your business.

GET HELP FROM OTHERS

Do you remember a time when you were a kid and you had to do something that was hard for you, like homework, cleaning your room, or anything that you had a challenge with? Your parents would ask if you needed help, and right away you would decline, saying it was easy for you and, yet, 15 minutes later you couldn't do it. You most likely had this happen to you before, and just like this applies to your personal life, this applies to many businesses around the world! They have a clear problem in front of them that they need to solve it but they're too scared to ask for help, or they think it's easy. A couple months later, or whenever it took them to solve their problem, they realized that they could've had a much easier time fixing the problem if they just accepted a little bit of help.

That happened to me personally, when my dad and me founded SAC. I wanted to bootstrap everything myself, without help from anyone. I soon came to the realization that it was way too hard for me at the time, and that I needed help from others. Whether it was getting people to donate to the organization, making a design for raffle tickets we were selling, or collecting toys from others, it started to get hard for me to do it on a big scale. I would then ask my dad for help, and after weeks or months later, we fixed most, if not all, of the challenges I faced that were really hard for me to do at the time. From then on, if I had a problem that was really hard, or something that I wanted to do on a big scale, I went to ask for help from others.

These are just my own challenges, but in reality this happens to millions of people that have a business. They don't want to ask for help because they're either embarrassed to ask for help, or they thought they could've fixed the problem they had very easily. You're going to encounter a lot of challenges in running a business; therefore, you're going to have a lot of problems that you can't fix and solve by yourself. So, it's to your advantage to ask for help if you can't fix some of the problems that come up.

Don't be afraid to ask for help. Most of you reading this, including me, at some point will be too scared to ask for help from others. For some people, they don't want to ask for help because of their pride. For others, they don't want to admit that they have a problem they can't fix themselves. Whatever challenge you're going to encounter in business that's too hard for you to fix by yourself, be willing to ask for help. This is also why people fail at their businesses; they have an opportunity to ask for help from others but decide not to. Later on, when they're trying to fix any challenge or problem, they have they realize that they should've asked for help when they had the chance, but now they feel dumb or stupid to ask for help, so they never do.

You're going to have challenges that come in a bunch of different sizes, big or small. It could be as big as getting a lawsuit from someone who's claiming your products or service is falsely marketed, and they're coming after you, or as small as accepting some documents that were late and now you need to present something to a client without them.

The whole point of this is to not be afraid to ask for help. Be willing to get help from others and don't be afraid if they're going to say no or that you're going to seem dumb because you can't fix the problem yourself. However, don't think that you should ask for help with everything. Remember that the opposite thing happens at times--you have a bunch of challenges that you don't think you can fix yourself, so you ask for help in every single one of them.

Some problems you're going to be able to fix on your own, and you're not going to have a problem fixing it. Don't feel that you needed to ask for help with every problem you're going to have. Some problems you have to do on your own because of personal information, or you're working on a new product that you can't make public yet, etc. I know that I might sound wierd saying that you should ask for help at some times but not at others.

Here's the simple version of it. You want to know the difference between needing help and knowing that you can fix a problem yourself without help. Why? Because there's going to be problems that you're going to have that you know you can fix by yourself, but you might not believe in yourself, so you ask for help when you could've fixed the problem, and could've done it even better that the person you asked for help.

You have to figure out if you have a problem that you can fix, or if it's a problem you truly need to get help with. In conclusion, asking for help isn't a bad thing. When needed, you should have the courage to say I need help and get it. Just remember that sometimes you get a problem that you can fix yourself--try to give it a shot first. Who knows, maybe you're going to solve it the best way you can.

COMPETITION IS GOOD...OR IS IT?

We've all heard it before, "Competition is good. It helps you improve yourself, your products, services, marketing, etc.," and although it's a great answer and a hard argument to fight against, let's look into it a bit more. When talking about competition in your business, sports, competition, fights, etc. it's obvious it's good and helps you improve. All of these things I talked about are true in almost everything you're trying to improve on.

For example, if you're an athlete trying to win a competition or trying to improve in general, competition would be good for you in that case. It encourages you to become the best you can be, to outperform everyone and yourself for the better. You have something to motivate you to train for whatever you're trying to win. I'm sounding like competition is so great and it's needed to win and improve in yourself and your business so far, right? Here's where everything changes. Although competition is great in some cases, like trying to win a sports competition, or trying to improve in a personal skill. It's one of the things that kills you in business.

In other words, COMPETETION = GOOD IN SPORTS, COMPETETION = GOOD IN MASTERING SKILLS, COMPETE-TION = BAD IN BUSINESSES. This might sound a bit crazy, but here's some more detail about it. If you have a business that has competition everywhere that's trying to kill your own business, that's stealing your customers, and saying bad things about your business, tell me you wouldn't want to get THEM out of business and keep their customers. You'll be the only person that's able to sell those products, and best of all, you'll have one less business to worry about that's trying to get YOU out of business.

This is exactly why you shouldn't want to have competition in running a business. What you should want to do instead, which is pretty obvious, but most people can't do, is destroying your competition instead of keeping them in business. I want to make something clear, however. Getting your competition out of business IS NOT EASY. It's never going to be easy unless your competition is clueless and you have a huge advantage. However, that's the whole point of having businesses! Some goals you'll want to have in your BUSINESS is becoming very profitable, become known, having many customers, and making it become hugely successful along with other things. How are you going to do that? **GETTING YOUR COMPETETION OUT OF BUSINESS!!!**

Yes, there are hundreds if not thousands of other factors to archieve those goals, but this is one of the most important things to do. In other words, if you don't destroy your competition or at the least get them way below your own business, you'll have a way harder time to be able to grow and become profitable. One of the biggest things your competition is keeping you from getting is more customers.

For example, let's say that I'm a local in the area and I'm interested refurnishing my house. We're talking buying new carpet, painting the whole house, getting a new roof, etc. Considering that I'm willing to pay whatever it takes for the best quality service. I'm guessing for everything I mentioned I wanted and a lot more, it's going to cost me $20K. I'm ready to hire a company to do it and now it's just time to search what company is the best at it. First off, I'm going to check online for the company's websites. That's where a lot of people fail right there. They either don't have a website or it may not look professional. They also might not have an app or a way to reach out to their customers online which is where the market is.

Aside from that, let's pretend that both you and your competition have a website. Now I have to see what each company offers, who is better in terms of quality, etc. Remember, I don't care about the price, so even if you have better prices than your competitors it's not going to make much of a difference. From there I now have to pick between you and your competitors. So, unless you have the best service, you have the same or high chance of not getting picked. Remember, it's not only you and another competitor; there are more companies willing to offer me even better services if I go just 5 more minutes from where I am right now. I'm choosing to pick one of your many competitors, and you just lost your chance of getting $20k of net income for your business.

Do you still think competition is good? How do you get rid of your competition then? That's the whole point of this chapter, isn't it? Well, the answer is that the whole book shows you how to get rid of your competition. This book talks about how to market yourself and your company, how to grow your business, it shows you the do's and don'ts of businesses and what to do when you encounter problems. The next part of the chapter explains the three best ways to make your company grow and to make it extremely successful, in turn there's going to be ways to outperform your competition and to make your business even more known than it is now.

THE THREE WAYS TO MAKE YOUR BUSINESS GROW AND BECOME EXTREMELY SUCCESSFUL

You're about to read a couple of stories about the best way to start a business on the right foot and how to make it grow! These stories are so simple, but so powerful at the same time, and it shows perfectly that the first step is hugely important if you want to start off with the right foot. This is one of the three things you have to invest in to be extremely successful in your company. I briefly mentioned my organization, Smiles Against Cancer (and what we do - we help put smiles on every kid's face that is battling cancer with a donation of toys).

In the beginning stages,and coming up with what would be SAC (referring to Smiles Against Cancer), my dad and I quickly determined what we were going to do, how we were going to do it, the hospital we were going to donate to, etc. After our first year, we made an impact of about $200 worth of toys.

It was a great step for us, especially because it was one of my first big successes not only in life but in business. The next year we stepped up our game by making a donation of about $500. It was a good year of donations for the kids, but we still felt that there was more we could've done. Right after we came back from the hospital we went to work. We started planning for the next year by looking at more possibilities for partnerships; more toys, creating attention to what we're doing, etc.

During the third year we took more action in creating

SAC's brand, and making more partnerships. We started selling chocolate bars to raise capital. I started to go to more events and places where I could connect with other people that could benefit me, as well as I could benefit them. I even went to MMA fights with a little stand selling chocolate bars and connecting with people.

After a couple of times going to MMA fights, I met a group of guys selling apparel. They were right next to my stand, so I approached them. We ended up having an amazing conversation about business and how can make both of our companies more successful. We ended up talking again later on. That same day we created a partnership and became good friends. Another time this year, I met David Hofmann, the president of the Rotary Club in Oakbrook. He was great mentor, and he taught be many lessons about business and the stock market. He let me speak at one of the Rotary Club meetings. I presented SAC to them and gave them my speech. A month later, SAC received a check for $800.

The next story is commonly known around the world and especially known in business. The Microsoft story; better yet how they came together. As some of you know, in 1990 Bill Gates attended Harvard University while studying a profession of business. Soon he decided to start a business which now it's known as Microsoft.

If you notice that so far, I've mentioned many examples of me meeting people whenever I could, and that's what one of the things you need to invest in to make your company successful, networking. You need to invest in networking with people anywhere and everywhere you can. Networking is "the action or process of interacting with others to exchange information and develop professional or social contacts".

Uber is easily one of the top transportation companies in the world, and it faces a real threat to taxi companies. It's valued at $75.5 billion. It's funny to think that they've only been around for 11 years and they're one of the biggest companies in their industry. You've probably been on an Uber before, and they offer a good service. It allows you to get a ride quickly for a good price, they're more reliable than taking a cab, and it's faster to get a hold of one than most transportation services.

Whether you love them or hate them, you and your neighbor know about them; however, what I want to talk about is how they started. It was founded by Travis Islamic and Garett Camp in 2009. Coincidentally, before they started Uber, they both sold a previous company they've had for millions of dollars. They met each other at a tech conference where weirdly enough they both had trouble getting a cab to the conference. Together they brainstormed an idea that offered a better and more reliable way to get a transportation vehicle, which later became Uber. They grew it enormously over time, and although they had struggles along the way, they finally made it become what it is today.

What's the takeaway in this story? Uber became what it is and changed the whole technology/transportation company, because two people networked with each other.

Both Travis and Garett met each other because they went to a conference that was meant to show people new technologies. Who do you think was going to show up at that conference, people who are interested in new technology or someone who doesn't know anything about technology/ doesn't want to know about it? People who are interested in new technology are going to show up and network with each other.

If that conference never happened, or if one of the two founders hadn't shown up, we most likely wouldn't have the new ways of transportation today. This can work for you too. If you want to start a business or want to get help with your own business, you should go and network with people who are interested and know about the areas you want to get into or need help from. It doesn't necessarily need to be a conference, because you have hundreds of ways you can meet people. Here are some of the best places you can network with people:

- Social media (Twitter, LinkedIn, FaceBook, Instagram, etc.)
- Associations/clubs (Boy Scouts of America, Rotary, Toastmasters, Freemasons, Key Club, etc.)
- Volunteering in communities you want to be part of

- Google/Ted Talk events
- Fundraising events
- Parks
- Festivals
- School
- Business organizations
- Tournaments
- Campuses
- Team sports

These are some of the many places you can meet and network with people but, generally, you want to look for places that offer meeting people that have the same interests as you and can help you as well as you helping them. Go to as many places that you can network in now because there's a possibility that you can find the next Zuckerberg of your time!

Networking is one of the most important things, not only in creating your business, or making it successful, but in anything. Networking creates new possibilities for you and your company that you would have never had otherwise. Once you network with other people, you'll always have a greater chance of meeting the client, partner, distributor, etc., you need and you'll be able to benefit them as well. Networking could be as easy as talking with people you don't know or going to a social event that has people you want to surround yourself with. Whenever you have the chance to network with other people, please do, even if you are skeptical.

On to the second investment you need to make your business successful. After you network with people, what are you going to do with them? Are you going to make them your clients directly, are you going to make a partnership with them, or are they going to get you a customer by recommendation? Whatever it may be, you need to make your decision quickly because they're not going to wait for you to tell them what they can help you with.

Once you've made your decision, you're somehow going to gain more customers from them. Now what are you going to do with your new customers? That's where the second investment you need to make comes in. **Every customer you come across shouldn't matter to you. It's only after you get your customers to come back and stay with you that they matter. Never let your customer leave, always find another way they can buy/benefit you.**

There's a movie called "The Wolf of Wall Street". It's a documentary/dark comedy film that shows the crazy life of Jordan Belfort (former stockbroker and now sales trainer). In the movie there's a scene where Mark Hanna (played by Mathew McConaughey) talks a young Jordan Belfort (played by Leonardo DiCaprio) in a fancy restaurant. As the conversation goes on Mark Hanna asks Jordan Belfort, "What do you do when your client buys stock at eight (starting stock price) and now sets in 16, do you let him cash out?"

Before Belfort can respond Hanna cuts him off and

responds with, "What do you do? You get another brilliant idea, a special idea...another stock to reinvest his earnings into." Whatever Jordan Belfort did in life, and whatever you might feel about the movie, that's a golden nugget that you can learn from. What Mark Hanna said in simpler way, is that once you get your clients, NEVER LET THEM GO! Always keep them buying from you, whichever way you can, legally.

For example, think of Coca-Cola. They always keep their customers buying from them again and again and again. How? They put an extremely high amount of sugar in their drinks to the point where an average coke drinker makes it a habit to have the drink. That is one of the many ways you can influence people to buy from you. Video games also get their customers to keep playing their game.

Fortnite became one of the biggest games in the country and in the world in a couple of years. They had an estimated earnings of $300 MILLION in the month of April 2019 and in 2020 they're looking to make even more money. Same as Coke, they make their users keep coming back to play every day. How? They add new places, guns, partnerships, challenges, etc. to the game. Because of that, Fortnite became the number one played game in 2020.

Another tactic to get people to keep buying from you again and again is by having collectibles and a continuation of products. Funko, Disney, Topps, Nike, book series (Harry Potter), Activision, etc. are companies who do this perfectly, and in turn make hundreds of millions or billions. All of the companies I mentioned have collectibles, or they sell a continuation of products that need other products for the full use (aka a book series, a game series, movie universes, etc.). The reason the tactics are so addicting to your customers is because they make them keep coming back for every product you release.

There are many ways to make your customers keep coming back to you and a lot of them come from marketing, advertising, promoting, etc. (more on that in Chapter 7). The lesson learned in your second investment to make your business successful, is always make your customers come back however you can, and keep them with you.

The third key investment you need for your business goes into making your corporate image. You've heard of Supreme, the clothing brand. If you know anything about them, you know their prices are RIDICULOUS. There was recent news that went viral--Supreme sold two OREO cookies for $96,000. That's CRAZY, why do people buy cookies in a package for almost $100,000 when you could get the exact same flavor, taste, and size in your local Wal-Mart? Why, because the brand of the company selling it had it made for themselves. Branding is one of the most important things a company has. It could make them the most powerful company in the world, or it could make them fail miserably.

Supreme made everyone think that buying a plain white t-shirt for hundreds of dollars makes the person feel more entitled than the guy sitting next to them wearing a $20 shirt from Nike. Another company that does the same thing is Gucci. Their quality of clothing is better than Supreme, but they still make their products overpriced. How do they get away with it? **By making their brand extremely powerful. They make their products seem as though only wealthy people could by it.** When you see Gucci, you think of hip, wealth, quality, etc. Not that the company itself is bad, but they make their brand powerful enough to make their prices anyway they want.

Thousands of companies do the same thing; they make their product seem like it's superior than their competitors. One of the biggest examples of this is Apple. They've made amazing things in the past such as the original MacBook, iPhone, and iPod, but recently they've only made minor changes to their products. They market them as the best thing since sliced bread. Just like Gucci and Supreme, they make the first thing that pops into people's head is quality, wealth, new, hip, accepted, etc.

Monopoly (the board game) also has an extremely recognizable brand. They've made the word MONOPLY a household name. Everyone knows what Monopoly is. Even you might have played it. They've partnered up with hundreds of TV shows, movies, games, books, etc to make their brand even bigger. Monopoly is in the top five bought board games in the WORLD.

Not only companies but people can make themselves a brand like Eminem, Justin Bieber, Flo Rider, Kevin Hart, Gary Vee, Arian Grande, Donald Trump, Katy Perry, Tony Robbins, Selena Gomez, Robert Downey Junior, etc. They've made their name popular around the world and now everybody knows it whether they like them or not. Companies that made their brand recognized around the world are Coca-Cola, Shell, McDonalds, Apple, Starbucks, Disney, Amazon, Visa, Six Flags, Tesla, eBay, Ford, etc.

In the world that we live in today it doesn't matter if you sell the best product in the world, instead it's who makes the buyer think that they have the better product than their competitor.

After you read the third key and main elements to make your business grow and be successful, what are you going to do? Each of these keys to success could and should be used in any stage of your business. However, if you're just getting started in your journey to make your business grow, then focus on key number one. Find the right people you need to start and take action. If you're a couple of years into your business, then focus on key number two.

Make sure to get your customers to come back to you, always and forever. If you're already in full throttle and you have experience in making your business grow, then focus on key number three. Make a brand for you and your company to make sure your customers know who you are. Before going into the next chapter remember, if you don't take action in what you learn, then it's not worth learning.

CHAPTER SIX

MARKETiNG/ADVERTiSiNG/ PROMOTiNG

"Doing business without advertising is like winking at a girl in the dark. You know what you are doing, but nobody else does."

~Steuart Henderson Britt

———————

DIFFERENCES BETWEEN MAP

Here are two options, pick either 1,000,000 dollars or 1,000,000 friends. This isn't a trick question, just two options. Which one would you pick? This question is HUGELY popular, not only in business, but in general. If you were to pick $1 million, it's a good choice. I'm not going to lie, $1 million is appealing, especially to someone who maybe didn't have that much money before, but comparing it to friends? I mean, come on, who would pick friends over a million dollars?

I heard that question a couple of years ago. I stopped, thought about it for a minute and I came to the conclusion that if I picked the friends, I'd be happy and well off, but a million dollars? I was 10 at the time, and to me, and I think any other kid at my age, a million dollars seemed better than getting a bunch of friends. Now, a couple of years after my first "encounter" with that question, I've learned more about business/marketing/sales and changed my answer. Yes, money is great, especially a million dollars for a kid. However, as I said earlier in Chapter 4, networking and meeting new people is one of the keys in making your business grow HUGELY.

Think about it in a big picture. If only one percent of your friends buy ONLY one thing from your business that, lets say, costs $100. One percent of a million friends is 10,000. Multiply that number buy 100. You just made $1,000,000. The second thing to make your business successful is keeping your clients. So, what are you going to do? Get the people who already bought from you to buy again. If they buy only a second time, you'll end up with $2,000,000! What if you could make those two options a reality? How? MAP. MAP-Marketing, Advertising, Promoting. Those three things are the center of how almost all the biggest companies in the world became what they are today.

To create your business into a massive company you need to get people to know who you are. How? Marketing is everything from advertising, promoting, corporate image, etc. The reason why it's called MAP is because, although everything falls into marketing, the top three things to make your business known is marketing, advertising, and promoting; and it's also catchy. Although you might not see it, you're always being brainwashed into thinking about a company's food, clothes, watches, games, products, etc. You see them on billboards, ads, memes, social media, and so much more. In the next sections of this chapter you'll learn what makes a certain type of MAP, and how you can use it to your advantage.

EVERYTHING FALLS INTO MARKETING

Let's dive right into it, what's marketing? Marketing is what everything falls into such as advertising, promoting, corporate image, social media, inbound and outbound marketing, etc. Think of everything like this. Volkswagen is a huge company and bigger than you think. They own Audi, Bugatti, Lamborghini, Bentley, SEAT, Porsche, Volkswagen, Ducati, SKODA, and a lot more. Marketing, just like Volkswagen, has a bunch of things

THE BIG IDEA - THE ROADMAP TO ENTREPRENEURSHIP

under the name. In VW's case, its cars, in marketing's case, it's ways to make your company known. Also like VW, whose car brands have different models, marketing has different models, too. For example, advertising brands is done on social media, radio, television, theater, etc.

Just like any other part of MAP marketing, they own "brands" (I'll be referring to things that are a part of MAP as "brands"). Such as inbound marketing, outbound marketing, digital marketing, social media marketing, video marketing, search engine marketing, relationship marketing and more. Although each of them are very important in their own way, in this book will be focusing on the top four "brands"--inbound marketing, outbound marketing, social media marketing, and video marketing. These are the top things in marketing to make your business known directly and indirectly, but either way it always gets people to notice you and your company.

Inbound and outbound marketing are what defines if you're going to wait for the cookies to come to you, or if you're going to find them. Think of inbound and outbound marketing like this, inbound marketing is, for example, you trying to sell a box of chocolates without creating any attention for you and your chocolates directly to consumers. However what you might do instead is create a blog or social media while talking about what your selling (in this case chocolate bars), and try to find customers in social media instead of going directly to your customer's houses or having a stand outside of your house. Inbound marketing requires less money to invest in and more of a waiting/patience game. Examples of inbound marketing are blogs, social media (YouTube, Instagram, FaceBook, TicTok, Twitter, LinkedIn, Snapchat, Pinterest, etc.), social media conferences, web-based seminars, interviews, podcasts, etc.

Inbound marketing is more of a defense marketing strategy, inbound marketing= appeal to your prospects without directly telling them. On the other side, there's outbound marketing. As always, there are many ways to sell your chocolates, but in the case of outbound marketing you're mainly going on offense instead of defense. Some examples of outbound marketing are TV commercials, sales calls, radio ads, press conferences, trade shows, direct emails, merchandise (both inbound and outbound marketing), etc. Unlike inbound marketing, you don't wait for your prospects to come to the table, instead you're putting your face anywhere and everywhere you can. Of course, for both inbound and outbound marketing there are always positives and negatives. In the case of inbound marketing the positives and negatives are:

PROS OF INBOUND MARKETING
-You can start without any money on a social media platform
-You have total control on what you market to your audience
-You generally have more time to say what you want to say to your customers, unlike outbound marketing you usually have a limited time to say what you want

CONS OF INBOUND MARKETING
-You'll most likely have a harder and longer time to reach your audience, unlike outbound marketing where you can immediately talk to your target audience
-You need to make more of an effort to appeal to your audience to make it work, whereas outbound marketing you give them information whether they like it or not
-You have the responsibility to post daily, unlike outbound the radio channel or ad host he or she will automatically do it for you

In the case of outbound marketing the positives and negative are:

PROS OF OUTBOUND MARKETING
-You have access to promote your product or service to the most popular shows, apps, or radio channels in the world
-You have the advantage to push your product out to your target audience immediately
-You're going to have a more offense strategy to your target audience than you would with inbound marketing

CONS OF OUTBOUND MARKETING
-You have to pay to get your word out there
-You can become annoying to whomever your marketing if they see your ad too many times, unlike inbound marketing the whole purpose of it is to make the customer come to you instead of you going to them
-You don't have much control on your ad, email or call, unlike inbound marketing you have total control of what you say/post

BE A JOKE (:

Marketing isn't all serious. Instead, you should have fun with it and come up with some crazy ideas on how you can market yourself. Some of the best ways to get people to notice you and your company (in other words, market yourself in a great way) is not surprisingly by making a joke about yourself. Let me further explain. I'm guessing that you're reading this and there's a high chance that you're a young teen or at least very into the social world. Therefore, you're mostly on big social media platforms like TicTok, Instagram, Snapchat, etc. Therefore, you're in a world full of memes. Which, by the way, everyone that uses all the platforms I've mentioned have a huge audience. One minute you'll see Charlie D'Amelio doing the renegade and the next you'll see the Cybertruck getting memed because of the broken window they had.

In case you live under a rock, or live in bikini bottom, what

I'm referring to is a launch that Tesla made that had bunch of other new vehicles released to the public's eye for the first time. The whole presentation was going well as well as the audience with people cheering Elon Musk on with each and every vehicle that he presented on screen. However, their biggest reveal was towards the end, which ended up being their new, fully electric truck named the Cybertruck. As expected, the whole audience was shocked because the whole time they're presenting the new truck, the audience was expecting a new truck or at least a very powerful vehicle.

Anyway, as Elon Musk was presenting the new truck and all its new features, mileage, price, etc., he finally got to the part of the demonstration that showed how the endurance and strength of the vehicle was; specifically the front side windows. To demonstrate how durable the car was, Elon brought up one of the workers at Tesla to the stage. Suddenly the audience was surprised that they saw presenter held a metal ball in his hand.

With the audience not knowing what he was going to do with it, Elon out of nowhere told the worker to hit the window of the truck directly in the middle. As instructed the worker threw the ball directly to the middle of the window and BAM! In front of millions of people watching the part of the widow that was hit was smashed and broken by the ball.

Everyone went silent, shocked that this happened in front of their eyes, and most of them began laughing at Tesla, but more specifically Elon. Before I get any further, I want you to think about this and the after effects of the fail. What do you think interested buyers of the truck would do, or think about their thought of buying the new truck?

Good, bad, or whatever, it is your right. Everyone in the country was disappointed, laughing, happy, sad, surprised, and most importantly; they were going to talk about it as much as they can. I personally remember when that happened. I was curious on the presentation and what they were going to reveal, so I decided to watch the presentation as soon as I could, and I was obviously having a good time watching all the products. Finally, the part of the presentation that was about Tesla's new truck was revealed, and in front of my eyes (or my phone) I saw the terrible malfunction the truck had.

My first reaction was being in a state of surprise but then I chuckled at it until the end of the presentation finished. I also want to state that I watched this happen no more than a couple hours after the video got published. I decided to watch YouTube for a bit and the very first thing I see in my explorer page was a thumbnail of a photoshopped Elon Musk crying, and the Cybertruck window cracked. No question, the video already had a couple of thousand views and a bunch of comments.

I watched the video and of course it was about the presentation and the part where the new Tesla's window was cracked. I laughed and went on to the trending part of YouTube where the first thing that popped up was a different video that I previously watched where the truck's window was getting cracked. It already had a couple million of views and to no surprise I clicked on it and a bunch of likes, dislikes, comments, shares, view, etc. Later as the day went on, I went on Instagram and saw a caption of meme's of the Cybertruck and the failure of its window.

I remember one meme in particular. It was a baby Elon Musk that was happy in front of the Cybertruck, right on the other side of the picture was a baby Elon Musk with the window that was cracked and he was crying. I died laughing (shows you my type of humor), and I knew that that the rest of the week, if not the month, was going to be filled with Elon Musk, Cybertruck, and Tesla failure memes. I then went onto every other social media platforms that you can think of and every single video was full of memes related to the fail of the Cybertruck.

The most important thing to note is that TicTok had a bunch of videos related to the failure of the truck and about one of every five videos had them. I kid you not. The sheer amount of anything related to Elon Musk, Tesla, or the Cybertruck was way too many to count. Soon my whole family and all of my friends were talking about it. I also want you remind you that this all happened in no more than a couple of days and there were already memes, videos, and reviews of the truck.

I wouldn't be surprised if there were fan clubs dedicated to the truck. A couple of weeks, if not a little more than a month, passed by, and Tesla released the availability to preorder the truck to the public. At this point I already was heavily into business and I knew that there were going to be huge amounts of orders for the truck that was going to be released because of the amount of publicity it got. I was expecting close to a couple hundred of people were going to pre-order the truck. When the media released how many pre-orders they got, I thought my mind was playing games on me. In front of me there was the report that Tesla had over ten thousand pre-orders. They translated the orders to how much they made and there was over $50 million that was made. $50 million Tesla made was made without spending a single dime on marketing, media, etc.

The craziest thing of it was that they haven't even sold one truck yet. You heard me right, they haven't even sold one truck yet and they already made $50 million dollars (all the trucks were preordered, not yet sold for the actual price). On top of that, Tesla didn't spend a single cent marketing their vehicles and they still got millions of dollars in return. How were they able to? They got much publicity and marketing just by getting made fun of.

To some of you old-timers or people who think there's only one way of getting your products or company marketed to the public (aka people who think that the stunt or accident that was pulled by Elon Musk only worked by sheer luck) this is not surprise that they became this successful. In the view of the public, Tesla became something funny but also had what everyone thought was the new thing, which it actually is, and

WHY IS DENTISTRY IMPORTANT?
Because even though he's missing an eyebrow, the first you notice is his SMILE!

it was something that was cool to everyone. This is something that should be taken more seriously in business marketing in general: the meme. The world is changing as I'm writing this and probably as you're reading this. The new ways that business and companies market themselves is going to change for better or worse.

The only way you'll become part of the trend, or the way you can use it for you and not against you, is by changing your marketing technique NOW. You, as well as companies all over the world, need to realize that if you want to become successful in marketing your product or service or even yourself, is by being willing to get made fun of, and to get into your buyers type of area. This is just one example of a company that got made fun of and there are countless other ones like Deltaco, Chipotle, etc. Use this to your advantage and notice that this is going to be way more effective than the traditional ways of marketing, like billboards or radio. THIS IS CHANGING!!

BE FUNNY ((:

Be funny, yet become creative. In the previous chapter we've talked about how to become creative and why it's important. Now it's the time to really use it to your advantage.

I know, I know. That picture is so silly and dumb, but I'm betting that it got a giggle out of you. For those of you listing to an audio book and not the book the picture that was shown is a picture/ad from a dentist that had a normal family of a man, wife, and kids. However, the first thing that you notice is that the man in the front of the picture was missing his two front teeth. On the top of the picture there's a caption that says, "The funny thing is the first thing you notice is a man missing his two front teeth, but what you don't notice is that his eyebrow is missing as well." At the bottom of the picture there is another caption that says, "This is why dentists are important."

Anyway, the whole point of the picture was to prove why dentists are important. No doubt the original dentist already got thousands of dollar's worth of appointments for people that need their teeth fixed. The picture went viral around the

internet and especially on Instagram, but the point is that this caught a bunch of people by surprise. I remember the first time I personally saw the picture. I was on my explore page on Instagram--I clicked on it and then I laughed and got the joke.

Why I want to bring up the picture (besides the obvious) is because I want to think of some ways that you can do this yourself. Whatever type of business you have, think of a way to make a joke of yourself or whatever you're selling and somewhere get a funny reason why they should buy your product. I know I'm sounding a bit bland, so let me give you an example of what I mean. Let's say that you have a pet company and you're trying to sell a vaccine for dogs. A good picture you can make is in the front of the picture you have a dog with a big wide smile while playing around on a grass field. However, on the dog's fur you can see a bunch of different little tics and creepy crawlies on the dog. Then on the top of the caption you should say that this is why you should get your dog a vaccine (you don't want him to get tics).

That's only one picture you can put on and market to your audience, but there's a bunch of other ones. Another picture you make for a vet is for a vaccine that's harmless for your pet and doesn't hurt them, like a pill instead of a vaccine. On the picture you'd put a picture of one dog in one side of the picture that's really sad and that clearly didn't like getting stung by the vaccine. On the other side you have a picture using your product (the vaccine pill) where the dog is really happy and cheerful.

Another example of having fun with a product, and specifically with their competitor, is Coca Cola. To give you the backstory, originally Pepsi put out a picture on Halloween that had a Pepsi can wrapped around by a cape that was a CocaCola cape. The caption that they put out said "Have a spooky Halloween" referring to coca cola as a scary product. It became a gag and it got some traction. Coca Cola got a bad rap, and everyone thought they just got dissed by Pepsi. However, a couple weeks' later Coca Cola released a picture that was exactly the same picture as the one Pepsi released. The only difference was that instead of the caption "Have a spooky Halloween," the caption read, "Everybody wants a hero." In other words, everyone want a Coke.

The picture exploded in popularity and hours later people were making fun of Pepsi and saying that they got roasted by Coca Cola. It was all over Instagram and most importantly almost everyone saw that picture and though to themselves,

236

"I want a Coke." That is something that a lot of big companies don't do, but instead do the opposite. Most companies would have some type of way to make their competitors seem bad or in other words, they would make fun of them.

The other company, instead of coming up with their own comeback, would get mad at the company and not speak about. Did Coke do that? Nope! They went for it and embraced them. If one of your competitors makes fun of you and they get some attention, don't take it so seriously. You should instead embrace the picture and use it to your advantage. Don't take it so seriously; instead, go with your own comeback. Heck, you can even be Pepsi in this situation.

You can be the first one to throw the punch and make fun of your competitor first (try to make it actually funny and relatable). Most of your competitors won't have a comeback to give to you but in case they do, do the same thing again; make fun of them. Again, the whole point of this is to market you in a way that people will think is funny and with a goal of making it go viral (especially in social media). Just remember, actually make it funny and relatable to your buyers. Don't make some of those cheesy ads that no one likes, and people just think that they're annoying instead of funny--you mainly see these on cable.

BECOME RELATABLE TO YOUR CUSTOMERS/ MAKE THEM LIKE YOU (((:

So, how do you become relatable to your customers? Better yet, how do you get your customers to like you and or your product? The best way to describe it is this. The way to become popular and get people to like your product is by getting someone to represent you or your company that's popular with your target audience. The most important thing to remember is to be open to everyone, EVERYONE.

Getting someone to represent your company is super easy, you just need to have the connections and the right network. That's easy. The hard part or the part that most companies are scared about, is getting someone who isn't to family friendly, or better yet, someone who isn't PG-13. Don't get me wrong, you don't need to always get someone who curses all the time, does inappropriate stuff, etc.

Disney, one of the biggest companies in the movie theater industry has a SUPER family friendly look and if they see, say, or do something that isn't in their family friendly picture, they'll immediately delete or make sure that it is deleted. However, Disney did recently buy Fox, and they're thinking of adding more adult content for their audience. So we'll see how that goes. Back to the point, the way to become relatable to your target audience is by getting someone they know and like.

One of the best companies that did this was Chipotle; in 2020 (the time of me writing this) they made a partnership with David Dobrek and his team (YouTubers/social media influencers) to give away a Chipotle lifetime card (free Chipotle for life) to people who were on either TicTok or Instagram. The way to win the card was by putting out a video that explained why you deserve to get the card. The best part about it was that anyone could enter, and anyone could win the card. The way Chipotle marketed their prize was with the help of David Dobrek. All he had to do was tell people how to win the card. In other words, he was the face of the partnership (besides Chipotle, of course). Now that you know how it worked, I want to show you how they got people to like Chipotle and how they became relatable to people.

The first thing that Chipotle did to make themselves relatable was by getting a person who teens and young adults know and like. David Dobrek was the first part and is someone everyone knows, especially kids all the way to young adults. He's someone who gets people to like him no matter who they are. You can be bored or having a bad day, but as soon as you see a David Dobrek vlog you'll feel better because of the positive attitude he gives off. He's relatable, likeable and most importantly known.

Chipotle could've picked a famous celebrity like Justin Bieber or Tom Holland, but they didn't. Why? It's because most people don't and can't relate to them. Unlike David, who is someone anyone can relate to (for those of you who don't know much about him you should check his YouTube vlogs out). Another way that he was relatable was because he's on almost every social media platform.

Most YouTubers or social media influencers are mainly only on one site more than every other one. The more your face or company is known, the better. The next part of the equation is being liked. Now, you may be asking yourself didn't Chipotle already choose someone who was well liked? Why stop there? Let's go further! So how could they make themselves and their brand more relatable? By basing their whole challenge or prize on being liked.

Think about it, when Chipotle, or better yet, David Dobrek, announced that to win the prize you need to explain why you deserved it. What would you do if you wanted to win a prize that required you to say why you need to win the prize? Well, I don't know about you, but I'd for sure say things that give me a higher chance of getting picked; I'm going to make sure I say things that make me likeable. I'm not going to make a video that's dedicated to winning a challenge and not saying anything that makes me likeable. I'm also going to make Chipotle seem likeable and praise it to be the number one fast food restaurant. So, almost all the videos that are made to try to win the challenge are going to have things that make both Chipotle and the challenger seem likable.

I forgot to mention that the amount of people trying to win the prize is practically all of TicTok (mostly in the U.S). So TicTok is bound to get thousands if not millions of videos that are related to Chipotle and people trying to win the card.

Therefore, there were millions of videos that are making Chipotle seem to be associated with being likeable. That's the second part of the equation. Which, by the way, THATS THE KEY! Chipotle made them relatable to their consumers and future customers by getting someone who's already relatable to all of their customers.

David Dobrek was the first part of the key to the equation. Then, to make themselves seem likeable, they geared the challenge that way. This is one of the best things I've seen a company do that was extremely successful and made them known. I could go even further, saying that each video needed someone eating a burrito from Chipotle to give them a higher chance of winning, but I think you get the point. Sadly, they never released how much Chipotle made from the challenge, but based on how many people participated in the challenge I'm 100 percent sure that they made a pretty penny during and after the challenge. Heck, it even worked on me. After I saw a bunch of videos made of Chipotle and people trying to win the challenge, I decided to make a video for the fun of it. But before I made it, I had to do something extremely important first, get a delicious huge burrito from Chipotle!

VALUE

What's the whole point of marketing? The whole point of marketing and its ultimate goal is to get more people to buy your product or service. Whether you're a B2B (business to business) or B2C (business to consumer), marketing is a vital part of your business, and if it isn't already, it had better be now. Again, your ultimate goal with marketing is to get more people buying from you. We've already gone through a couple marketing strategies and how to approach them, but what do they all do, no matter what? They all grab attention from your buyers.

For Chipotle they wanted to grab attention from teens to adults, for Coca Cola, they were trying to get the attention from Pepsi's users, and for the picture of the dentist, they were trying to get attention from people who don't think dentists are important. So, how do you get people or business's attention?

It's by creating value for your prospects. If you somewhat understood the main things in business before reading his book, you should know that this is the most basic and common answer when asking how do you grab people attention in marketing/business. And it's 100 percent true. Of course, there are different techniques on how to grab attention, which is all this chapter is about, but here's a deep dive and a further explanation. Think about any business there is in the whole world. Every single business's main purpose is to get customers. That's their whole purpose as a business. Here's a graph that's shows exactly what each business offers to their customers.

- Fast food franchises+Values=Food for people's hunger

- Eye care companies+Values=Care for people's eyes

- Amusment parks+Values=Rides for people's amusement

- Technology companies+Values=Technology for people's life
- Real estate companies+Values=Homes for people's shelter needs
- Music industry+Values=Music for people

These are different values that companies or industries provide for their customers. The reason I wanted to talk about the different values companies provide is because that's exactly what you need to do to get people's attention, and how to hook them in. Your business's whole purpose is to create value to people or businesses in its own way. What does this have to do with marketing? This has to do with marketing because whichever way you market your product or service to your customers is always based around the value you're going to give to them.

This is the most important thing you need to keep in mind when creating a marketing strategy; it always has been based around the value you're going to create for the people you're marketing to. It's not required to base EVERYTHING on the values you give, but you'll have a way better time selling your product or service when you do marketing. Always try getting people to notice and clearly see the value you're selling to people. That's one of the problems that I mention in Chapter 5.

When Apple had too many products, people didn't realize what their main value was and how/why they should buy it from them. Now, they're all better and are doing extremely well, but they had to struggle in order to get to the point they're at now. What if you don't know what the value is of the product/service you're marketing to consumers? Very simple, do your research.

If you ever start to get confused on what your company's main thing to prioritize should be, you should do research on your company's products and service to see what's the top selling thing. One of the greatest movies in business, *The Founder,* has some of the greatest business scenes ever. One scene in particular is around the beginning of the movie when Ray Kroc went to take the McDonalds brothers to dinner to hear their story. As they were explaining to Kroc their ups and downs, they mentioned that their first business was failing and they had to figure out how to become profitable. So, they did their research and figured out that their top selling products were burgers, fries, and shakes.

At the time they were selling all kinds of stuff like chicken, corn on the cob, and turkey, along with burgers, but what they hadn't figured out was that there were too many options to choose from for their customers. They stopped selling every single one of their products except the ones I just mentioned--burgers, fries, and shakes. You may be saying that's a simple scene and it's not that valuable. However, it is that simple.

The reason why is because this shows exactly what you should do if you end up having too many different things that you're trying to sell. All you've got to do is your research. See what your top selling products are, their profits and losses, how much they sell, and how little they sell. Maybe one product sells less than another, but maybe it's way more profitable than every other product. You need to do your research and see what you want focus on. After you do, I'm guaranteeing that you're going to have a way better time seeing what you want to prioritize. Also, even if you do your research and figure out that one product is not doing as well as the other products, it doesn't mean that you're not going to be able to fix it.

You can't ever forget the why of a product or service. Figure out what products are most profitable. See if one product has potential by figuring out the why and execute on it by fixing the solution. Maybe you see the why and it's not worth your time, then dump it. You need to do your research if you want to figure out the main thing to prioritize and become your business's main value.

This is also what any grocery/shopping center does. If you ever see an item on sale or on clearance at Wal-Mart, it's for a reason. It's because they do their research and see if a product is worth selling not. If it's worth selling they're most likely not going to sell it on clearance or on sale besides some rare occasion, like black Friday. On the other side, if you see an item on clearance, it's mainly because the product is not doing well and they're willing to make less profit in order to get rid of it and make room for other products.

In all, you need to make sure your value in whatever you're selling is clear and worth people buying. This is a perfect quote that explains why you need to clearly show your business value.

"People love to buy, but they never like to get sold." That's little phrase is so great because it's TRUE!

The reason why this has to do with values is because you want to make your values stand out in a way that people never think they're getting sold to. If your value is truly helpful (or at least people think it's helpful) you'll have a way easier time selling whatever it is you're selling and marketing. For example, if you get a bunch of people buying from you without the requirement of sales people you'll know that your values are true and they're worth people buying. Make sure your value stands out and make sure they're important to people and their needs.

In conclusion, marketing is a huge part of business, but it's truly very simple. Marketing is something that to be successful with, you need to be creative with it. Most people think that marketing is something you need to take very seriously and it's something that you can't have fun with, but in reality, it's the complete opposite. Marketing is something that you need to have fun with, and you should truly enjoy both in business and in your life.

Have fun with it. Have the courage to say to a bunch of other corporate types that we need to be innovating and we need to be creative, and forgot about the traditional ways of doing things. I know that I keep saying fun and creative over and over again, but I can't help it. Yes, you need to be professional about it, but you need to be CREATIVE AND HAVE FUN WITH IT!

"Remember that marketing is fun and creative, however most people don't think it is. Have fun with it and become creative with it." By Alexander Jimenez. Marketing is something cool and awesome that you can't resist liking. If you don't, something's wrong with you.

CONCLUSION

This whole book has been a journey for me as well as for you. We've gone through marketing, business advice, school, the willingness to change, and so much more! I'm going to keep the end of this book short because, let's face it, a lot of authors, when writing books, add WAY too much at the end of the book. So, I'll leave you with two things to take away from this book if you can take anything.

One, TIME. Time is the most valuable asset we have and it's way too precious to let go of and to waste. Without time you're nothing. Without time you wouldn't have the basic necessities of life. Without time the world would be a whole different place. **TIME is the most valuable thing ever.**

The last thing I'll leave you with is action. Action is the single most important thing to creating success in your life. This entire book is completely useless if you don't take action. Action makes or breaks any goals, admirations, day-to-day things, and so much more. Remember this quote for the rest of your life and you'll be set. "Action with the use of time is the most powerful thing you can have to create anything you want in your life."

~Alexander Jimenez

BUSINESS TERMINOLOGY GLOSSARY

Accounting = The process of recording financial transactions pertaining to a business.

Angle Investor = A high net worth individual who provides financial backing for small startups or entrepreneurs, typically in exchange for ownership equity in the company.

Assets = A resource with economic value that an individual, corporation, or country owns or controls with the expectation that it will provide a future benefit.

Balance Sheet = This key financial document provides a snapshot of business assets, liabilities and owner's equity.

Bankruptcy = A legal process which happens when a person, company, or organization does not have enough money to pay all of its debts.

Bookkeeping = A method of accounting that involves the timely recording of all financial transactions for the business.

Bootstrapping = Using your own money to finance the start-up and growth of your small business. Think of it as being your own investor.

Business Plan = How a business, usually a startup defines its objectives and how it is to go about achieving its goals.

Buy In = An agreement to purchase shares of something, in some cases to buy a stake in a company that also has

THE BIG IDEA - THE ROADMAP TO ENTREPRENEURSHIP

other owners.

B2B = A form of transaction between businesses.

B2C = A form of transaction between a business to a customer.

Capital = The overall wealth of a business as demonstrated by its cash accounts, assets, and investments.

Cash Flow = The amount of operating cash that "flows" through the business and affects the business's liquidity.

Collateral = Any asset that you pledge as security for a loan instrument is called collateral.

Depreciation = The value of any asset can be said to depreciate when it loses some of that value in increments over time

Debt = Amount of money borrowed by one party from another.

Employee = Someone who gets paid to work for a person or company.

Equity = The value that would be returned to a company's shareholders if all of the assets were liquidated and all of the company's debts were paid off.

Franchise = Opportunity from a company that allows a you to start your own business legally using someone else's (the franchisor's) ideas.

Financial Statements= Written records that convey the business activities and the financial performance of a company.

Liability = Something a person or company owes,

usually a sum of money. In other words, something that a company/ person owns that's taking money away from them instead of making money for them.

Liquidity = Something a person or company owes, usually a sum of money.

P&L = Profit/loss a company or person has, makes, or loses.

R&D = Research and development a company/person does to a new product or service that they're about to release.

ABOUT THE AUTHOR

Alex Jimenez is a 13-year old with grit. His business acumen is inspiring and now, after starting his own successful nonprofit and being exposed to entrepreneurship from an early age, he is ready to share his passion and knowledge with other young entrepreneurs.

He most recently entered the TIME Kid of the Year 2020 competition and created an impressive nomination video as a pitch for the TIME young entrepreneur competition that can be viewed on his website. The history of business has been around since the dawn of humanity—from cavemen trading pelts and food to the 21st-century method of super-fast e-commerce. Business and entrepreneurship are fixtures in our daily lives. It's not just adults that find these topics of interest. Younger generations also want to get in on this game from the bottom up is limited to their classroom with educators who are not entrepreneurs themselves. Alexander Jimenez, the author of The Big Idea and a teenager himself, saw that young people like him crave information about business and entrepreneurial basics.

FROM THE AUTHOR'S POINT OF VIEW...

"The way that most schools teach the subject of business to kids is sadly not as valuable compared to the many available resources. Schools need to teach this topic with a serious yet friendly approach. Today, anyone—including teens—can find answers to their business questions from experts. However, these answers can be hard to comprehend and would require simple explanations. I chose to write this book to help my young readers learn about business easily and simply so they can understand."

Alexander's book speaks to young readers by introducing them to the foundations of marketing, business strategies, challenges and solutions to creating and building a business, leadership, and getting the upper hand over the competition. Although dedicated to children and teenagers, this book applies to anyone who wants to know the basics of business and thinks of becoming entrepreneurs. Alexander wants readers to be excited about learning key business and leadership principles that will serve as personal roadmaps to entrepreneurship.

www.ingramcontent.com/pod-product-compliance
Lightning Source LLC
Chambersburg PA
CBHW071540200326
41519CB00021BB/6555